TRANSYLVANIA

THE LAND BEYOND THE FOREST

Transylvania

THE LAND BEYOND THE FOREST

BY

LOUIS C. CORNISH

Hon. D. Pol. Sc.
Royal University of Hungary, Szeged

DORRANCE & COMPANY
PHILADELPHIA

REPORTS OF ANGLO-AMERICAN COMMISSIONS SENT TO
TRANSYLVANIA, COMPILED BY LOUIS C. CORNISH:
(BEACON PRESS)

"TRANSYLVANIA IN 1922," BOSTON, 1923, PP. 169.
"THE RELIGIOUS MINORITIES IN TRANSYLVANIA,"
BOSTON, 1925, PP. 174.

CONTENTS

FOREWORD

In the summer of 1944 Russia and Roumania agreed that all Transylvania should be given to Roumania, and in September, 1944, Russia, Great Britain, and the United States, signed an armistice with Roumania at Moscow confirming this decision, but making it subject to the later approval of the Peace Conference. Its final form may be long in coming, but whatever it may be it will prove of pivotal importance for Central Europe and for the peace of the world.

What about it?

Europe is a unit creating its own form of life which in the course of its development cannot but become a single community.

PAUL TELEKI.

I

THE MENACE

TRANSYLVANIA GROANS in her anguish. Her ancient civilization is being ground away. Make no mistake, we are involved.

If organized peace is to be one and indivisible, and for this great end more than forty nations have fought a world war, being the largest coalition for peace the world has seen,* then fires cannot be left smouldering to flare again. Transylvania is a world danger spot, strategic and desperately important. Because it presents one of the thorniest political problems in Europe, indeed in the world, we cannot ignore it. For the world's protection the United Nations, soon or late, has got to grapple with it.

It is a waste of time to discuss the decisions made after the First World War. What matters now is to correct mistakes, for the sake of all the peoples involved, and for the moment not to mind too much just what political form the correction takes. The future concerns us, not the past. Emphatically this is the business of America as one of the peace planning nations, and also because at Yalta the United States, together with her two partners, took "joint

* With Denmark's admission on May 29, 1945, fifty nations were represented at the San Francisco Conference.

responsibility" for establishing lasting peace in Europe on a just basis and by democratic methods.

First of all look at the situation broadly. There are spots on the earth's surface most potent in man's destiny and Transylvania is one of them. If Britain lost the Faulkland Islands perhaps it would count for little internationally, but it would be a mighty affair if she lost Gibraltar. If the United States lost an island off the coast of Maine she would not be deeply affected, but if she lost the Panama Canal, as the Axis planned, geographically a small area, she would live in terror. Hungary is strategic. In Central Europe she is pivotal. Transylvania, for centuries her easternmost part, is also strategic. Hungary, long a bulwark of western civilization, now has sinister international significance because of her dismemberment following the First World War, and the problem what to do about it. She lost two-thirds of her whole area. Transylvania, torn from her old allegiance and given to Roumania, ever since has been shouting her wrongs; not perhaps because of her love for Hungary so much as because of her unhappiness under Roumanian rule. For twenty-five years Roumanian misrule has shown that a mistake was made in ceding Transylvania to Roumania. Basic in these matters her geographical unity was ignored, which strangled her economy. Quite as urgent, Roumania has flouted her pledges for the fair treatment of her minority peoples. So the problem what to do about the future is fraught with dangerous possibilities.

She is a beautiful land, this Transylvania, a land of wide plains surrounded by mountains, and served by abundant streams and rivers. Long, deep valleys with their tumbling waters lead to the timbered uplands, and these in turn give

place to the high encircling mountains, among them—on
the east—the blue Carpathians. She is a very loveable land,
commanding the devoted allegiance of all her peoples. We
hear the Saxons singing,

> "Transylvania, our sweet country
> Our dear fatherland,
> Be thou saluted in thy beauty
> And about all thy sons
> May the bond of unity be twined!"*

She is a land of villages. When Saxon they are German
in appearance; when Roumanian they resemble those on
the south side of the mountains; when Magyar they are
like those in other parts of Hungary. Yet all of them, Magyar, Saxon, and Roumanian, have distinctive Transylvanian quality. The three peoples, despite difference in descent, are loyal Transylvanians: in a mysterious way the
villages carry the impress of the land itself.

We remember particularly the Magyar villages, with their
white stucco houses and their red tiled roofs, standing beside the well-shaded, winding streets. Wide, highly colored
gateways open to the enclosures. Ancient churches stand at
the centers, sometimes still surrounded by their fortress
walls built in the old days against the Turks. From the high
towers sounds the music of many bells. Nearby are the
schools, and yonder the colleges. Before the First World
War these ancient villages of the "nations," despite many
periods of upheaval, were places of quiet plenty. In them
or their like, here and hereabouts, have lived the Magyars
for a thousand years, the Roumanians for a very long time

* See chapter on the Saxons, p. 208.

stretching back perhaps to the days of the first settlements, we would avoid entering on the Dacian theory of Roumanian descent, and the Saxons for six hundred years.

Where is this fair land of Transylvania, so little known to Americans? It lies at the far eastern edge of our western civilization, the defense of which has been its history. The great currents of western thought, in education, science, and religion, always have penetrated throughout Hungary and Transylvania, its former easternmost part, but always they have stopped at the Carpathians. Western learning, hammered out with infinite toil and pain, came early to Transylvania, but it never crossed the mountains. She has been for centuries the easternmost outpost of Western European civilization. For example she was the first nation in the world, she was at the time an independent principality, to pass laws protecting religious freedom so that within her borders no man thereafter should be persecuted for his religious opinions. This was in 1568, and was in sharp contrast to the laws and customs of the rest of Europe.* Is the high western civilization of Transylvania to be rubbed out in eastern Europe? Are the United Nations going to let it be rubbed out?

We cannot remain aloof. This problem is emphatically American business, if for no other reason than our own self defense in avoiding the slaughter of our men in continuing wars. The United States cannot but be deeply concerned over the permanent pacification of troubled southeastern Europe, where other wars may start unless there are effective readjustments.

* Transylvania proclaimed religious freedom at Torda in 1568; it was forced on Roumania only in 1878 by the Treaty of Berlin when she was freed from Turkey, and never has she practiced it.

What political form such readjustments should take is in endless dispute. It is generally assumed that there are only two alternatives, Transylvania must belong either to Hungary or to Roumania; to Hungary because with fluctuations it was Hungarian for a thousand years; to Roumania because Roumanians were among the early settlers in the region, and more because they now form a majority of the population. Hungarian or Roumanian rule, these two alternatives, have monopolized attention.

There is a third alternative, however, the collaboration or federation of at least some of the Danubian states in which an autonomous Transylvania would be included. Such a drawing together of neighboring states might have happened in the past except for interference from outside. "No part of the world has suffered more from the meddling of individual great powers," says John MacCormac. "What economics had joined together imperialist politics were always pulling asunder, and the result did not make for peace. That used to be the rule. If justice is to be done to Middle Europe it must be permitted and encouraged to federate."*

The third alternative, then, is to allow Transylvania to become an autonomous part of a Danubian Federation, let her become a state within a framework larger than her own independency, like the states of Switzerland or of the North American Union. She was an independent principality for a century and a half during the Turkish invasion. Shut within her mountains she always has been conscious of her peculiar unity.

All three Transylvanian alternatives, since the Federated Nations meeting at San Francisco agreed to oversee troubled areas, are touched with a new light, for we hope that

* News release, London, March 3, 1945.

we are witnessing the beginning of a new world order. Certainly there is new hope for the third alternative, joining up Transylvania with a Danubian Federation, for the International Organization which the United Nations are building cannot but profoundly influence the future of Transylvania. In the Versailles decisions there was a forever-and-ever quality, only mitigated at the start by an attempt to guard the rights of the minorities. The Trianon Treaty provided for the protection of the Transylvanian minority peoples given to Roumania, but unfortunately Roumania did not keep her pledges, and under the setup of the League of Nations no method was available, or workable, for the League's continuous oversight, and for changes when they were proven necessary. It may be that in the stress of the hour and the general ignorance about the values and problems that were involved in decisions, the peace makers at the Trianon expected too much of the semi-oriental Roumanians who had been established in their own independency by the Treaty of Berlin only since 1878, a nation hardly half a century old at the time of the Trianon Treaty. This is written only in an attempt to understand, not to blame.

When Roumania's failure to protect her minority peoples continued on and on and became clear to all the world beyond any possibility of disproof, the minorities themselves together with their friends took the only next step then possible, they laid the minority sufferings in Transylvania before the Council of the League of Nations and asked for help. Nothing happened. Nothing could happen. Now we all know and only too well—remembering as we must Japan and Manchuria, Italy and Ethiopia—that the League of

Nations lacked power, due to weakness in its setup as well as to international conditions.

The League could only decide on such matters by unanimous consent, and Roumania supported by the system of the Little Entente always could find ways and means to prevent unanimous consent, and in this way to postpone the protection of the Transylvanian minorities indefinitely. Unfortunately these tactics became the general practice of the League regarding the protection of the minorities everywhere. This not only left the minorities unprotected by the League, but it weakened the League itself by weakening the world's confidence in its powers. Let it be repeated, this evasion of great responsibilities for protecting minorities—due to weakness in setup or lack of wisdom and courage among its leaders, call it whatever you please—was a chief cause of its decreasing moral authority among the nations. Sabotage of protection for the minorities under its protection was a never ending charge made increasingly against it. The League had accepted the duty of protecting minorities as provided in the treaties, and the word duty was in the original Tittoni resolution. Criticism has rained on the founders of the League for not planning better for minority protection, but in a time of great difficulty in starting the League no doubt they did the best they could. It is to be remembered that world parliaments are but of yesterday; paths through international rivalries and ignorance are hard indeed to hew. Anyway all this is of the past. World conflagrations have burned away much stubble. Vast operations have happened since the days of Trianon. Joint international parliamentary procedures which the United Nations set up have greatly improved the whole world situation. We kindle our torches of hope anew.

The new world organization, instead of holding meetings only at stated periods, as did the League, is to function all the time. Many adjustments on procedure were settled in San Francisco, and from the start our United Nations organization will run more smoothly. The armistice terms, between Roumania and the United Nations, state explicitly that Roumanian rule in Transylvania is subject to the approval of the Peace Conference.

How efficient the machinery of the United Nations will be in the early years of the world parliament is anybody's guess, but unless the United Nations can oversee and review decisions regarding Transylvania and similar situations, as may be needed to create stability and peace, then their sons killed in this war will have died in vain. It is for the United Nations, for all of us, mightily to resolve.

So the long continuing Transylvanian problem reappears, as dire for world peace as it has been of late years, but not without new hope of betterment. And new hope rests wholly on getting to the world public a worldwide knowledge of the tangled realities of the Transylvanian situation. It matters supremely for world peace that this great pivotal territory be well governed, and allowed to develop. Fires of discord must be quenched. The whole world must come to know the problem, for while it is intricate it is not insoluble. We must know at least in outline the events which have led to the present situation.

In 1916 the secret treaty of Bucharest, often called "the worst of the secret treaties," promised Transylvania to Roumania if she would enter the First World War on the side of the Allies. It was a desperate time in the struggle, those in power thought it essential to prevent Roumania from joining the Axis. The promise was given by the Allies and was fulfilled at the Trianon Treaty. The "Inquiry Report" of the American experts later called this treaty "a product of evil diplomacy" preventing "a just or lasting settlement of tangled problems." Against the advice of experts Transylvania was given to Roumania, but with safeguards for protecting the minorities. In 1940, a quarter of a century after, when the Russians were marching into Bessarabia and Moldavia, and the Hungarian army was mobilized on the Roumanian frontier, Hitler's need to keep possession of Roumanian oil uncomplicated by an Hungarian-Roumanian war forced Roumania to return the northern part of Transylvania to Hungary. In 1944, when at the eleventh hour Roumania deserted the Axis and joined the Allies, not voluntarily for Russian armies were at her gates, Russia promised her the whole of Transylvania. By the end of 1944 all of Transylvania had been occupied by the Red Army. Gradually parts of Russian-occupied Transylvania were handed over to Roumania. Immediately Roumanian armed bands began looting minority property and spread a reign of terror. These chaotic conditions induced the Red Army to interfere, and temporarily it took over administrative responsibility. This time the minority peoples of Transylvania were saved by the Red Army. We can but wonder how affairs will go when the Roumanians are alone in charge. Until better days come it will be the responsibility of Bucharest.

After the First World War Hungary lost 71% of her entire realm, 60% of her arable land, 90% of her forests, 75% of her meadows and pastures, and 63.6% of her population. It was dead low tide. Then in 1938 restorations began. The tide had turned. From Czechoslovakia, Roumania, and Jugoslavia together, a total of 52.9% of her former realm with predominantly Magyar population and 60.9% of Hungary proper was returned, and her population rose 14.69 million souls.* These revisions of the Trianon adjustments have now been reversed again, so we are told; but perhaps the end is not yet for the United Nations is an implemented world organization for review.

It is not surprising that all Hungarians rejoiced in August, 1940, when Roumania gave back the northern 40% of Transylvania to Hungary. It looked then as if the tide was coming in. The general assumption was that Hungarian rule, at least in the returned part, would permanently continue. Observe, it was generally taken for granted that the future rule in Transylvania has only the two familiar alternatives, she would of course belong either to Hungary or Roumania. But this conclusion is a non-sequitur.

A quarter of a century of hate-provoking experience of Bucharest misrule has been shared by all the peoples of Transylvania. All of them have been exploited. If these conditions continue, it cannot be denied that they threaten the peace of Transylvania, and so of the world. Stability in Transylvania never will be attained by allowing Hungary or Roumania alternately to be top dog.

Besides a small scattering of other peoples there are but three Transylvanian "nations": the largest group Roumanian, next in size the Magyar, and the smallest the Saxon.† A governmental solution must be found that will be acceptable to all the three peoples; difficult, yes, but by no means impossible. For the sake of stability and peace it is idle to talk of giving Transylvania back to Hungary. The Roumanians, who form the largest single group, will

---

* Statistics by Dezso Laky, "Companion to Hungarian Studies," p. 13.
† The Szekeley nation we include with the Magyars.

not willingly live again under the Magyar rule. As a road to peace it is idle to discuss giving it back to Roumania. She has tried to obliterate the minorities; such is her practice, and purpose, and mentality. We are presenting the facts without prejudice. The worst accusations against Bucharest rule in Transylvania come from the long resident Transylvanian Roumanians.

Why not make Transylvania autonomous? This was Kossuth's solution; he held that there was no other solution of the problem of Central Europe except a Danubian Federation with Transylvania a part of it, and many men have agreed with him.

Again, what about it?

II

WHERE IS TRANSYLVANIA?

TRANSYLVANIA LIES on the far eastern edge of Europe on
a line between the Gulf of Finland and the Black Sea. Some
authorities divide Europe and Asia by this imaginary line
beginning at Lake Ladoga, and running southward through
White Russia and the Ukraine. The Lake lies eastward
from the end of the Gulf of Finland, on the map not far east
of Stalingrad. The line ends at the Black Sea, let us say at
Odessa, just north of the coast of Bessarabia.

Toward the north it crosses cold, rough country inhos-
pitable to the wandering nomads who in early days were
ever trekking westward from the Russian steppes. Somewhere midway on the line they had to face the high Carpathians. Small groups might penetrate them, and the lesser
ranges which rise behind them, and might even manage to
ford the many rushing mountain streams that would meet
them at every turn. They might get through the dense and
far extending forests, and so arrive at last at the Central
Plain; but it was impossible for large companies of migrants, encumbered as they must have been with cattle and
goods, to follow this mountain route. They were forced instead to keep on southward, round the corner where the

Carpathians bend abruptly to the west, and follow this comparatively easier way into Europe.

Take note of the great natural barrier, the Carpathians. They have been of vast historical importance. Sheltered behind them lies Transylvania at the very center of our imaginary line dividing Eastern Europe from Asia. All of Hungary is a basin protected by encircling mountains, impassable for large companies of men on the east, but passable for them on the west. The very citadel of this great enclosure is Transylvania, from the earliest times a fortress for western Europe against the East. In all the world there is no other natural fortress like it: it is unique. By way of demonstration lift your left arm to a horizontal position, bend your forearm toward your shoulder; from your elbow to your hand your forearm slopes to the northwest and represents the Carpathians. From your elbow to your body your arm runs east and west, and represents the Fogaras and other Alps. Inside your elbow lies Transylvania. From your body to your elbow, for the moment "the corner of the Carpathians," the mountains present a barrier six hundred miles long and penetrated by only ten passes. This barrier still divides Transylvania and Roumania geographically. In the northwest, west and southwest rise other mountains, difficult though not impassable.

When in 1944 the Russian Army invaded Hungary the main forces marched through the Focsani gate, which had been opened for them by the Roumanian Army, and then marched south of the Carpathians around Transylvania and westward to pass through the Iron Gates of the Danube. They put light forces into the passes leading into Transylvania to guard against surprise attacks on their flanks. Another Russian army at the same time invaded Hungary on the north of Transylvania, across the "wooded Carpathians" that constitute Ruthenia. Observe that the Russian General Staff had come to the same conclusion arrived at by Genghis Khan in 1242. When passing over these same two roads he developed the same pincers movement, both spearheads being directed against the Capitol, now called Budapest. Despite modern technical developments, it is evident that the Transylvania Bastion has not lost its strategic importance. A major army still prefers to follow a far longer but smoother route to the south avoiding Transylvania rather than struggle through her impossible mountains.

Along this route from the east and around the corner of the Carpathians came the Hungarians, or Magyars, the names are interchangeable, at the end of the ninth century. After stops along the way, they settled in what has since been known as the Hungarian Plain. Soon after their arrival some of them again turned eastward, following up the valleys, through the forest belts, and settled permanently within the shelter of the mountains in what they called "the land beyond the forest," Transylvania.

All Hungary is geographically a unit. Her mountains, her river systems, her plains or basins, and her valleys make her one, and Transylvania is an integral geographical part of her, with a character of her own, an area of 22,312 square miles, and a population of 2,678,367. Her geographical unity makes Transylvania also economically a unit. Her very livelihood depends upon her interdependent agricultural and industrial regions, her mountains and valleys and plains, which have to exchange their products freely. Because of economic laws this unity is inescapable. Further, her mixed population is so thoroughly mixed that it is impossible to divide her ethnically, a condition which under stable rule may yet prove to be her strength rather than her undoing. To divide her economic and geographical unities, as has been shown, cannot be done without ruinous consequences. Protected by her mountains, bound together by economic necessity, she has always been a unit until recent years, and despite ruinous conditions she remains a unit today. Only united can she serve her self-supported economy, and her colorful high standard of civilization.

Fate has given her no mean role to play among the nations. Her position is far more than latitude and longitude. Not only does she lie on the far eastern edge of Europe, she is the strategic spot where the east meets the west. To the east, southeast and south, live peoples who have been dominated by the Orient. Transylvania, together with all of Hungary, early gave allegiance to the west and adopted western Christianity. On her fifteenth century coat of arms the turul, her heraldic bird, turns his head away from the Mohammedan crescent and looks to the cultural sun or light of the west, a charming heraldic symbolism and profoundly true in Transylvanian history. In her battling for the west Hungary, and especially her eastern portion Transylvania, earned the titles "defender of the west" and "shield of Christianity." Transylvania never could be grouped with the "waste headlands of the earth." Preeminently placed for the defense of western European civilization from the inroads of the East, which once was pagan, then predominantly Moslem, and now is predominantly Greek Orthodox, Transylvania persistently has fought for western civilization. She even has repeatedly attempted to carry western thought, science, medicine, tolerance for differences in religion, into the Orient.*

Transylvania through the centuries has been closely akin to Hungary even when politically severed. During the Turkish Invasion for a century and a half she was an independent principality; after the war with Austria she was part of Austria but not of Hungary. Despite these interludes she has been integrated with the larger history of the Magyar people. To the end that we may understand Transylvania, we have first to understand the Hungarians. To comprehend something of Transylvania's importance we have to see her relationship to Hungarian history, in which she is literally embedded.

* For a full account of Transylvania's position within Hungary and in Europe, see the Chapter by Count Paul Teleki, p. 239.

III

WHO ARE THE HUNGARIANS?

THEY FIRST appear faintly far away and long ago, when China defeated the Huns about 50 B.C. and smashed their empire. It was an epochal event believed to have started the great migration of Asiatic peoples toward Europe over the vast plains, which stretch interminably westward from Manchuria to the Carpathians. Against them China had built her wall, and Rome had established her *Limes*. Now they were on the move, great waves of them, Germanic peoples, the Hunnish tribes, the Avars, and among the last the Magyars, who began their migrations perhaps before the fifth century.

Their field for roving was vast indeed. To the extreme east lay the Chinese Empire. To the west the Roman, following the Rhine and Danube Rivers. The west of Hungary, often known as Transdanubia or Pannonia, was part of Rome's protective zone established against them. Between the two empires there were many other barbarian tribes, moving endlessly about in search of grass and water for their cattle and horses. The Magyars were "hard riding, nomadic Turkic peoples." When they emerged into history, they had a well-developed social, political and military organization. Throughout their long trek of some four centuries, they had no doubt done much fighting. They had lived under several "empires," shifting political masses but slightly coordinated.

At the end of the ninth century they arrived in the region between the Dnieper and the lower Danube, which they called "Etelkoz," a continuation of the great Eastern Plain that stretches toward the Balkans. It has been given different names in its different parts—Cumania, later Wallachia, Moldavia, and finally Roumania, the country which the Berlin Congress created in 1878. The region for centuries had been the last camping ground of northern and eastern peoples making their way toward the Roman provinces, Goths, Huns, Avars, and South Slavs, Bulgars and Magyars. Open to attack from three sides, it was hard to defend. All the migrants stayed only for a time and then moved on. All of them went around the mountains, and did not get into Transylvania, except the Magyars. The final thrust that drove them westward is said to have been given by the Petchenegs, an Asiatic people from the Steppes. Driven on no doubt by many forces they arrived on the Carpathian plain, now Hungary, after some four hundred years of formative tough living. They had become a hard fighting, upstanding, disciplined people.

Such in outline is the accepted belief about the origin of the Magyars, supported by Byzantine and Arabic reports, by mediaeval chronicles and, perhaps the most important evidence, by the Magyar language.

Even for those of us who have little knowledge the linguistic field is fascinating. The Hungarian words concerning cattle raising, for example, have Turkic origin, showing where the nomads learned part of the art. From all this study a considerable historical picture emerges, and certain kinships are established. Says Barczi,* "Hungarian is a Finno-Ugrian language, its closest relations being Vogul, Ostiak, Suryene, Votiak, Cheremis, Mordvin, Estonian, Finnish, and Lapp." Completely isolated in Central Europe, the Magyar language doubtless will yield many more racial secrets as its intensive study continues.

All authorities, however, do not agree. "The opinion that the Magyars are of preponderantly Asiatic, Mongol stock can be dismissed in the light of anthropological research. They are a mixed race . . . and may rightly be termed a people of European racial composition," says Kosary. And Count Stephen Zichy after ably presenting the probabilities of Magyar origin, admits that "these conclusions are hypothetical."

While we are not ignorant of the differences of opinion, we have no wish to enter on their discussion. The Asiatic origin of the Magyars is generally accepted by competent historians, and by philologists. We can do no other than believe that the Magyars, mixed with races whom they had contacted in their long trek of centuries, came to Hungary from the Russian Steppes, and at the end of the ninth century arrived at their mountain guarded land that ever since has borne their name. There they settled permanently.

They had entered a circular territory, protected by mountains, a unique geographical entity. "Within this Carpathian basin," says Kosary, "one may define certain transitions of territory, rather than separate regions of different character. Only Transylvania may be treated as a distinct entity within a larger one." The first settlements were on the plain; only a short time later some of the people as-

* Geza Barczi, professor of Philology at University of Debrecen, Hungary, "Companion to Hungarian Studies," p. 272.

cended the valleys, threaded the forests, crossed the central mountains, and entered Transylvania.

All the seven tribes of Magyars together were not a large nation. Zarek claims that they numbered no more than the people of modern Oxford and Cambridge. Perhaps they were fewer than the scattered inhabitants whom they found. But they were outstanding. Leo the Wise of Byzantium wrote of them, "This people abounds in men and is independent. Aside from their love of pomp and abundant life, their chief aim is to fight bravely against any invader." They had need of their courage.

They had taken over the Carpathian basin, at the time of their coming called an "empty" land. There had been inhabitants in the past, the Avars and others, but fortunately for the Magyars when they arrived the country was but sparsely inhabited. Fugitive remnants of the former occupying peoples, it is true, had hidden themselves in the mountains, or had formed tiny settlements; but all of them together had established no kind of state. Nominally they were under the Bulgarians. They now joined with the newcomers, who we are told had left their villages unharmed. They may have joined willingly; except for the Magyars they were unprotected. Few and scattered over the great spaces of Hungary, these remnants of the earlier settlers amounted to little. The Chronicler Procopius tells us, speaking of the Byzantine troops who had to cross the land, "They were oppressed by hunger when going through that region devoid of men."* According to Einhart, Charlemagne's biographer, the land had been empty for a hundred years. How fortunate, we say, were the Magyars to find an empty land, and one of such rich expanses, abundant

* Otto Zarek, History of Hungary, p. 49.

waters, and protecting mountains. Later chroniclers saw in it the Hand of God. But just how fortunate were they?

In every direction stretched lands that were far from being empty. And there was enmity. The long period of the migration of peoples from east to west had come to an end. New states were rising, especially powerful among them Byzantium and the great empire of the Franks. All the nations were fighting their neighbors and dreaming of conquest. None of them wanted more turbulent Asiatic tribes settling within their fluctuating borders. The saturation point on newcomers had been reached.

The empty land was theirs for the taking; yes, but could the Magyars keep it? To the north the Slavic tribes settled in Bohemia were already planning to occupy the empty land themselves. To the south, other Slavic peoples, the Croats and Serbs, were reaching northward. Not only did the Magyars stand between these two dangerous probabilities of attack, but all around them, to the east over the mountains, to the northwest beyond Bohemia, indeed in all directions, were peoples who when they dared were ready to wrest from the Magyars this beautiful land they were making their own. Two alternatives offered; they could await attack, and then let battle decide whether they should be free men or slaves; or they could attack first before their enemies struck. Their decision is revealing; they attacked. They loved to fight!

It is an amazing drama. The Magyars had only come into Europe just before the gates shut. They had entered an empty land, rich with fertile plains, and mighty forests, protected by rugged mountains. Now, the long trek ended, it would seem that they might settle down and be at peace. No chronicler tells us whether they cried happily, "At last!

18417

At last!" Or whether they made more arrows and mended their leather armor. Probably they did the last! The people outside naturally wanted to get in. So the Magyars, these mere newcomers, these barbarians, girded themselves, mounted their fast horses, which they excelled in breeding, they were the first to use stirrups, and proceeded to sweep through Central Italy, through France, even into Spain, collecting loot, making allies of strong peoples who feared them, establishing themselves among the settled peoples of Europe whom other peoples would do well either to let alone or make their friends. And this fighting campaign, or raiding habit, they continued for a century.

Their fighting showed adaptation and courage. Their light shields were covered with leather. It was their only protection both for horses and men. Their enemies wore metal, overburdened their horses, and were not as fleet or as mobile. Of course the time came when their enemies developed strategy, and victories were not so easy. Of course they had their defeats. They were badly beaten by the Germans in 933 and again in 955. So they stopped raiding to the West and instead raided to the East. But they had established themselves. They had won their place. The Magyars counted in Europe.

We get a glimpse of them in action. An ancient chronicle tells of their raid on the great monastery at St. Gallen in Switzerland.

News was brought to the monks that the Hungarians were coming. "They at once transported their most valuable belongings to a neighboring stronghold and took refuge there themselves. The Hungarians found the monastery deserted except for a single monk, who—as he himself states—could not follow his brethren, because the prior had forgotten to supply him with shoes. Heribald, as he was called, awaited the Hungarians without fear. When, to their surprise, he was discovered, they tried with the help of an interpreter to find out what he was waiting for, and why he had not escaped. He told them. The Hungarians laughed heartily at his story and did him no harm. Heribald was soon quite at home among them. The soldiers began questioning him about their valuables. He showed them the door of the treasury which they immediately broke open. Except for a few objects not worth carrying away, it was empty. Disappointed the soldiers threatened to flog Heribald, but finally let him go and continued their search. Two casks of wine were discovered. Having plenty of their own, a soldier began knocking away the hoops on one of the casks to let the wine flow. 'Spare the wine, my good fellow,' said Heribald. 'What are we to drink when you are gone?' The soldier desisted and told the others to let the casks alone. The soldiers sat down in the courtyard of the monastery and began to make merry. Heribald took part in the revelry, declaring afterward that he had never partaken of such good meats and wines. After the feast the soldiers took to shouting and singing, and forced Heribald and another monk who had been taken prisoner elsewhere to sing also. Dancing, wrestling and jousting followed, to show the captains their prowess. But suddenly came the sound of horns. In a twinkling the soldiers had seized their arms."*

This took place in 926, only thirty years after the Magyars had arrived in their Carpathian basin.

* Abbreviated, page 17 from "A History of Hungary," by Imre Lukinich.

IV

EARLY MAGYAR HISTORY

ONE OF the great monuments of the world stands in Budapest, if the Germans did not destroy it, the Millenery Column, erected in honor of a thousand years of Hungary's life. It is a slender shaft surmounted by an angel, and surrounded by equestrian statues, chief among them that of Prince Arpad, who led the Magyars from the lower lands into the Carpathian Plain. Arpad's character is strongly portrayed, mounted on his horse he is unforgettable.

Europe's future in no small degree depended on him and his people. All the nations were in flux, all were fighting and dreaming of conquest, boundaries waved to and fro, new tribes were a danger. Was Arpad with his Magyars friend or foe to struggling Christianity then but insecurely established along the western marches of Europe, and bravely preached by missionaries who often were martyrs? The Prince could have known nothing about the influences determining the future of Europe, but he was by no means the least among them. He was upsetting the European balance of power, such as it was. Two pagan peoples had invaded Europe, the Norsemen and the Moors. About the time he came the Norsemen were at Paris. Would the Magyars permanently belong to the Asiatic hordes from whom they had emerged? Did their coming mean that the East was permeating Central Europe? Would they settle in Western Europe and stay? Would its feeble civilization survive? Arpad could have understood none of these matters; yet had his people remained pagan, and given their loyalties to the East, European history would have developed very differently. The ninth and tenth centuries were crucial.

In the high Rocky Mountains a little brooklet divides. Part of it flows eastward and eventually reaches the Gulf of Mexico and the Atlantic. It is the beginning of the Mississippi River. The other part, the beginning of the Columbia River, flows to the Pacific. With a paddle you can guide a floating leaf either to the east or the west, toward the Atlantic or the Pacific. Every traveller stops for a moment to play the part of fate. Headwaters are always fascinating. So to stand by the splendid bronze statue of Prince Arpad, his face looking gravely into the far future, is to be at the European headwaters of Magyar history.

Within two generations of Arpad the life of Europe for the Magyars focused sharply. His great-grandson Geza turned to the west for affiliation. He sent word to the German Emperor, Otto the III, that he sought peace and would welcome Christian missionaries; doubtless the Emperor was pleased with both messages. A young and idealistic man himself, supporter of the Pope's dream of a world-inclusive Christian empire to be ruled by Pope and Emperor, here new strength was offered him for the cause. Plainly it would be better to live at peace with the Magyars than to fight them, so he sent messages and missionaries accompanied by German knights, who, as time passed, gained influence at the Hungarian Court.

It was given to Geza's son, King Stephen, only twelve

years old upon the death of his father, to become a Christian, and by precept and example win the people to the new faith. Throughout his long reign of forty-one years, 997-1038, he labored to make his Magyars followers of Christ, and he diligently promoted closer relations with the West.

Perhaps with a shrewd desire to please the Emperor as well as the Pope, he asked the Pope to confirm his Christian royalty by giving him a crown. The request was granted, and by special envoy the Pope sent him the crown that ever since has been used in Hungary, and after Stephen was canonized became known as the "Holy Crown of St. Stephen."* It was placed upon Stephen's head on Christmas Day in the year 1000 and with additions it has remained as the Pope gave it. It is the symbol of remarkable unity and stability sheltered in the territory within the mountains, that has proved to be one of the most stable boundaries in all Europe. What the surrounding seas have been to Britain, and the Pyrenees to Spain, her mountain barriers have been to Hungary. They made her center one territory after the Turks were expelled until Stephen's realm was torn asunder again by the Trianon Treaty—a colossal error for which the United States, through its representatives at Versailles, is by no means irresponsible. If only Austria-Hungary could have been made part of a larger federation, instead of being broken into small pieces—well, we might not be where we are today! But we are engaged with fascinating old King Stephen, and we would listen to his "admonitions to his son" which give us a measure of the man. "If you wish the honor of kingship, be peace-loving," he tells Prince Imre. "Rule over all without anger, pride or hatred, but with love, tenderness, and humility. Remember always that

* See Chapter Louis Kossuth, p. 64.

each one of us has the same standing; nothing exalts a man but humility; nothing humiliates more than haughtiness and hatred. . . . Peace-loving monarchs rule, the rest only tyrannize. Be patient toward all, influential and destitute alike."

His contemporaries say that Stephen was merciful to his defeated enemies, offered shelter to countless refugees, in short, that he kept these Christian rules himself. He was a strong King, governed firmly, and his diplomacy extended well over Central Europe.

Among those whom he sheltered in their exile were two English princes, Edward and Edmund Ironside, the last descendants of Alfred the Great, whom Canute had sent to Sweden to be killed. The Swedish king instead passed them on to the Hungarian Court. Edward is believed to have married King Stephen's daughter Agatha, and their daughter to have married Malcolm, and so she became St. Margaret of Scotland.

From St. Stephen's time down to our own there have been a bewildering number of Hungarian kings; twenty-four of his own dynasty in the first two centuries after him, in the next two and a quarter centuries fourteen, and seventeen from 1526 to 1920. British reigns have been averaged with edifying conclusions about the stability of the British throne. It is equally edifying that these fifty-five Hungarian kings averaged reigns of seventeen years each, periods longer than the British kings. They ruled from 1000 to 1920 with many vicissitudes. These nine hundred and fifty years since St. Stephen's time have seen great fluctuations. What nation indeed has not felt the mighty swing of the tides? Yet all along amazing stability has been shown in Hungary, derived from the geographical position within its protecting mountains, and also from the Magyar character. Through all this time, let it be repeated, Hungary has been wedged between the northern and southern Slavs, between the Empires of the East and the West, between the followers of Jesus and Mohammed, between the Orient and the Occident.

Cardinal Peter Pazmany wrote to Gabriel Bethlen in 1636, "We are squeezed between two powerful empires like a finger between folding doors." This is not strong enough. It might be better to say that they were always being ground between the upper and nether millstones. In 1566 the old Sultan Suleiman crossed the Hungarian frontier for the seventh time. "The Holy Roman and the Byzantine Emperors, the Sultans of the Ottoman Empire and the Hapsburg monarchs," says Julius Szekfu,* "for centuries tried everything in their power to subjugate this lone tribe. The Magyars were few indeed, but they never surrendered. Century after century they fought desperate struggles against superior forces. Their reward was that Hungary became known as the bulwark of Christianity."

Before considering this grinding we mention three of the intervals when Hungary had no king. John Hunyadi, ruler of Transylvania, whose name became famous throughout Europe for his successful campaigns against the Turks, was governor (Kormanzzo) of the whole realm for six years, 1446–1452; Louis Kossuth, champion of freedom, was governor for one year, 1848–49, and Admiral Nicholas Horthy was governor of the mutilated kingdom from 1920 through the very hard years until March 19, 1944, when Hitler took over the Hungarian government.

When the Magyars were being ground they stood alone.

* Dominic Kosary, History of Hungary, p. viii.

Such is the way of life, perhaps it could not have been otherwise. Yet there is something very moving in the Magyar
fight against great odds. The Asiatic invaders were bent on
conquering all Europe. The Magyars blocked their path.
Bela IV (1235–1270) points out to Pope Innocent IV that
the protection of the Danubian territories against the peril
of a second Mongolian invasion in 1253 is the concern of
all Europe, but that the Magyars get no assistance in their
battles "except words." Long afterwards Hunyadi writes to
another Pope, "We are in the sixtieth year of the struggle
against the Turk. Until now only one people has turned its
arms against the enemy. We only,* left alone, have endured
the fury of the battle." "We can either free Europe from
the cruel Turk's invasion, or we can fail for Christianity,
earning a crown of martyrdom."‡

There was an enormous accumulation of spiritual values
in Western Europe, and of material values as well, which we
call European civilization. There was much to tempt the
Turks to invasion, Hungary blocked them. She was, of
course, first of all fighting for herself, but in doing this she
was also protecting Western Europe. At any time she could
have made good terms with the Turks by letting them pass.
Instead she was incredibly devastated and depopulated.
More than half her land, after the Turks had occupied her
central portion for a hundred and fifty years, was uninhabited. When at last they were driven out she had to resettle
these areas with foreigners. Eighty per cent of her Magyar
people had been killed or sent into slavery.** This was the
period when the predominantly Magyar character of Tran-

* Lands to the south had fought. He refers to the European nations for
whom Hungary was a protection.
‡ Dominic Kosary, "History of Hungary," p. 64.
** Ibid., p. 62.

sylvania was lost. The tragedy of Trianon can be traced back through its many ramifications to the extinction of Magyars during and after the Turkish wars.

No one forgets that the peoples to the south of Hungary also bravely resisted the Turks and paid terrifically. In 1371 combinations of Serbs and Bulgars were crushed by the Turks. In 1391 Wallachia appears on the register of Turkish vassal states.*

Unprotected by high mountains as was Hungary, these nations were less able to withstand the invaders. Once conquered, their level lands offered an open road to Hungary, and beyond Hungary lay all Europe. Almost annually the Turks followed this broad highway over the conquered lands, and for eighty years Hungary blocked them. In vain the Magyars looked to Western Europe for help. They received only "words."

How the Magyars have paid and paid for their "empty" land at the junction of Occident and Orient! How they have been ground in its defense! They paid the Turks, and the Austrians. After the First World War they paid by their country's dismemberment. If the Russian-Roumanian Armistice terms stand, after the Second World War the lands that had been reallocated to Hungary are to be taken away, and Transylvania, briefly reunited to Hungary, is to be sacrificed anew to Roumania. The Moscow Armistice terms instruct, they do not authorize, they order, the Roumanians to intern the Germans ("Saxons") and Magyars. The Saxons have lived in Transylvania for about six hundred years, the Magyars for about a thousand. It is reported that the Saxons are already being deported to Siberia (April 1945). Britain and the United States assented to the Armistice.

* Seton Watson, History of Rumania, p. 33.

Roumania states, "The Government and the High Command of Roumania undertake to carry out measures for the internment of civilians of both above mentioned powers (Hungarians and Germans) who are now living there." No less than two million Magyars live in Roumania and Transylvania, and about six hundred thousand Saxons. Their sheer numbers may make the inclusion of them all in internment camps impossible. We can only hope that Roumania will stay her hand.

V

THE GOLDEN BULL

COMMENTS DEROGATORY to parliamentary systems in general were made before Count Paul Teleki, then Prime Minister of Hungary. He replied, "We Magyars had parliamentary sittings before we had seats; we met on horseback and discussed public affairs from the saddle. We will continue this ancient habit."

He packed all Hungarian history into his brief statement. The right of open discussion had been guarded and continued from the very beginning. For centuries it belonged to all the members of the original tribes; but with the gradual infiltration of feudalism from Germany it needed to be reaffirmed in order that the common people should be protected in their heritage of representation and freedom. So it came about that the Golden Bull was issued.

In all that it stood for and accomplished it relates Hungary fundamentally to the United Nations, for all of them revere the law. If this seems too clear a statement, compare them with their enemies, absolutist governments which ignore law. Our congresses and parliaments enact laws to express the will and wisdom of whole peoples, also they constantly adapt the principles of law to her occasions. We detest absolutism in all its forms. We want government by law. We have been fighting to sustain and extend it. Said Lincoln in his Gettysburg address—"that government by law may not perish . . ." This suits our reason and our sentiments, it is sound reason and sound sense.

Our basic respect for law in the United States flowers architecturally in our State capitols, all of them touched with grandeur. Apparently we feel that if we Americans are to be lavish in our building and symbolic, let it be here! See Lincoln, Nebraska, and Albany, New York. True, for convenience sake we take the elevators, but all of us love the pink marble staircases leading up to the law courts (Albany Capitol). True again, sometimes we ridicule a law, or condemn it bitterly, and often we change it. But this in the main is as it should be. To adapt law marks our struggle to keep it close to our moving life.

These reflections lead us back to law's origin. In the dim dawn of cooperation between men the strong man leads, what he decides on is accepted, but even so he must interpret the will of his fellows; if he gets too far ahead of them, or too far away on the left or right, or if he lags behind them, his leadership will end. So precedents get established, and followed, and finally are written down as law. In later days when life becomes more coherent the King oppresses the nobles, or the nobles oppress the King; or both oppress the people. Can all of them win their way through conflicting interests to adjustment? Progress, the very life of the nation, depends on adjustment; and adjustment gets written down and becomes law. There often is an urge in these matters that cannot be denied, provided the people have the stuff in them.

We can put a dam across a stream, but if it is powerful enough it breaks the dam and rushes on. Royalty can thwart a nation, but if the people are strong enough royalty opens the sluiceway and relieves the pressure, or sometimes the dam bursts and royalty is swept away.

Back in 1214, on November 4th, at Bury St. Edmunds, the British barons faced King John, and refused to pay him his scutage. After he had left, they solemnly swore together that they would withdraw their allegiance from him unless he gave them a charter. They did not trust royal promises, they wanted a writing! A fight followed at Runnymede where the King lost. So he opened the sluiceways; he gave the barons their writing known as the Magna Carta, signing it at London on June 4th, 1215.

We must briefly recall its provisions for it is the foundation of British and American law. We in the United States legally derive from it through our British law in early Colonial times, so does Canada, so do the other members of the British Commonwealth of Nations. Its influence has radiated on and on. Here in briefest form are its provisions:

  I Guarantees free elections to the church (in place of royal dictation).
 II Concerns inheritances, and chiefly affects the barons.
III Principally affects the subtenants and freemen, but also the barons.
 IV Benefits towns and trade.
  V Reforms judicial and legal matters.
 VI Restrains abuses by local officials.
VII Reforms administration of the forests.
VIII Deals with passing conditions; the Scotch and Welsh hostages are to be returned, certain mercenary soldiers with their followers are to be sent

away, and other immediate matters taken care of.

IX Appoints a self perpetuating committee of the Barons to see that the provisions of the Charter are carried out.

If it seems meager, and mostly to favor the privileged, we have to remember that it was written in 1215.

Having signed the Charter the King fought his Barons, but died in October, 1216, during the struggle. Whereupon the great compact was revised. Ever since, revision of the statutes has been the habit of peoples moved by the will to freedom, until naturally enough the towering edifice of statute law, of writings to defend all the people, of adjustments, obscure the cornerstone, the compact of 1215. Men died to defeat it, men died to sustain it, and, fortunately for free nations, the sustainers won.

Several original copies were made and signed, three survive. As we look at the yellow parchment and the finely written Latin script we wonder who was the author. No doubt a number of men contributed to its compilation, but history assigns the real authorship to Stephen Langton, then Archbishop of Canterbury, a man of wisdom and wide influence. To his gates came many travellers of note. Among those who visited him in 1220 was the Primate of Hungary.

What did these leaders of widely separated peoples talk about as they sat before the fire in the big hall of the Archbishop's house at Canterbury? Both had the will to freedom: maybe they discussed the Magna Carta! How indeed could they have avoided it being who they were? We are almost convinced that discussions of freedom for the church from royal dictation must have taken place, and maybe of other freedoms. However all this may have been, the Hungarian primate went back to his home in the land beyond the forest protected by the mountains, and two years later, in 1222, we have the Golden Bull. We know also that the Hungarian Bishop Eger spent several months with some of the Barons of the Magna Carta during the siege of Damietta, a port of Egypt, and no doubt the Bishop and the Barons talked of it. News travelled far even in those distant days, many besides the Barons and Bishops talked of the English royal writings for the protection of liberty. Influential as these contacts of men of high estate may have been, influences deeper in the life of the plain Hungarian people brought about the guarantee of freedom from the King to the people contained in the Golden Bull, widely known as the Hungarian Magna Carta.

Dissatisfaction had long existed in the country between two groups of people, particularly in the second decade of the thirteenth century. The large landowners distrusted the influence of the friends of the King. This situation is partly responsible for focusing affairs so that the King was forced to grant the Bull.

Of far greater importance was the shifting of relative importance between the large landowners and the great number of the lower nobility, together with the freemen living on the King's estates. In the thirty years before the Golden Bull was issued the large landowners had possessed themselves of ever more property taken from the King, and the lesser nobles and freemen accordingly came increasingly under their power, and then came drama.

Says Szekfu, "It was customary since St. Stephen that the kings held court once yearly at Fehervar, when everybody was permitted to submit his case to the King. This court was usually held on August 20th. But in 1222, upon general demand, another court was held in early spring in order to make it possible for the lower nobility, which cultivated its land without servants, and for all the free men who were not nobles, to appear. The Pope Honorius gives us a description of this National Assembly: 'The tremendous crowd, disregarding all commands of reasonable modesty, demanded all kinds of hard and unjustified things from their King.' And the King, being afraid that resistance 'might cause wild upheaval, dismissed his government.' Acting under the pressure of the Assembly, he issued the Golden Bull, whereby 'the liberties of the noblemen and of the other inhabitants of the country, acquired and decreed by King St. Stephen but unduly disregarded since, were confirmed.' "*

By these acts the lesser nobles were protected, and the freemen also were equally protected. The whole history of the assembly shows that those present transformed it from a crowd seeking justice into a real National Assembly exercising its political prerogative. In fact the Assembly succeeded in imposing on the King the rule that if his official family, especially the first official of the court, were to violate the rights assured to the people by the Golden Bull, they would be deprived of their office in the Assembly which was to be held yearly by the nobility and the other freemen of the court. Transylvanians were prominent in all these constitutional efforts, which took place in 1222, eight years after the Magna Carta.

Meeting different conditions in England and Hungary, the Golden Bull and the Magna Carta differ in detail. But despite this they are closely related in origins and purpose.

* Szekfu, Vol. I, p. 495. Abbreviated.

Both bulls expressed the free spirit of strong men when such expressions were new; both promoted self government and improved conditions for the common man. Both were the beginnings of constitutional government, and through the centuries have remained its basis in the two countries.

The name Golden Bull is hardly descriptive and, unexplained, might be misleading. It means only that this bull, or pronouncement, bore a golden seal. The Bull was the product of influences that had long been at work. It expressed the Magyar will to freedom, of which the Tripartitum, or great Law Book, is the most notable, for all the law of the Hungarian State rested on it for three centuries, and parts of it are still valid.

The Magyar will to freedom down through the centuries has found countless expressions. For example, even in the early days these people elected kings from members of the deceased king's family. The king-candidate for the throne had to await the verdict of the people. He "ordered" and "commanded" but only with the advice of his council. The witnesses are legion. Again for example, Bishop Otto of Freising testifies in the 12th century, "The Hungarians never make a decision in any important matter without thorough and prolonged discussion." St. Stephen's psychology of government, he reigned from 1000 to 1038, is as sound today, as living, as when he wrote it for his son. "It is counsel which creates kings, good advice administers the state, defends the country, wins battles, calls in our friends and removes the foe."*

The Golden Bull begins with a striking confession of royal shortcomings: "Andrew, by the Grace of God, King

* Companion to Hungarian Studies.

of Hungary, Dalmatia, Croatia, Rama, Serbia, Galicia, and Lodomeria: As the freedom established by King Stephen the Saint for the noblemen and other people of Our Realm, has mostly been reduced by the arbitrary will of several Kings, who sometimes exercised revenge when in anger, and sometimes listened to the advice of wicked or selfish persons, Our Nobles often assailed Our Majesty with many prayers to transform Our Realm." Having thus courteously cleared the decks without mentioning any shortcomings of the King's subjects, the Bull proceeded. The right of direct appeal to the Kings is granted. The National Assembly is to be summoned annually on St. Stephen's Day, August 20, instead of intermittently at the King's pleasure. Noblemen may not be imprisoned without judicial examination and sentence. This is the Hungarian "Habeas Corpus," naturally first limited to the lords, and later extended. The King gives up the right to enter the houses and villages of the nobles without invitation, thereby relinquishing the position of omnipotent ruler and becoming again, as in the ancient Blood Agreement, *primus inter pares,* first among equals.

The concluding provision, Article 31, is broadly significant of the people's consciousness of power. It is the *jus resistendi,* "If either We Ourselves or One of our Successors (so the Bull makes the King declare) should wish to counteract any of these regulations, this Bull entitles the Bishops, as well as the other Magnates and Nobles of Our Realm, together and individually, freely to oppose and contradict Us or Our Successors, without becoming guilty of high treason." Nine years later, when reformulating the Golden Bull, the King withdrew this clause, no doubt feeling that he had granted too much. Nonetheless the nobles and the people, with fluctuating results, continued to criticise as they were moved.

The Magna Carta and the Golden Bull are expressions of national wills to freedom. They spring from the same source, and serve the same end. The records of both countries are rich in individual declarations of this same mighty will.

"Be of good comfort, Master Ridley, and play the man," we hear the Bishop of Worcester, Hugh Latimer, calling to the Bishop of London, when both men were chained to stakes in Oxford and the fagots heaped around them were being lighted. "Be of good comfort. By God's grace we shall this day light such a candle in England as shall never be put out."

The same will to freedom speaks in the famous words of Francis David, Unitarian Bishop of Transylvania, 1510–1579, who before he died a prisoner in Deva Castle scratched on the wall of his cell, "Men may delay but cannot prevent the coming of freedom for all the sons of men, for freedom is the gift of God."*

Latimer and Ridley were burned in Oxford, October 16, 1556. Francis David died in Deva Castle, November 15, 1579.

After the compromise of 1867 Hungary, the smaller country, was attached to Austria, the larger state, the Magyars constantly stressed their copartnership, and pointed to their constitution. When association with Austria ended after the First World War, the Constitutional Government of Hungary, which never had lapsed, continued to function.

* Given the author by Bishop Ferencz and also by Bishop Boros of Transylvania.

Constitutional forms changed through the years in Hungary as in England. In both countries the rights protected by law were flouted and fought for. Indeed, what did Charles the First of England care about the constitutional rights of his people? But Oliver Cromwell cared mightily. So in Hungary there were periods of stress. In both countries through woe and havoc the people stuck to their constitutions.

This is perhaps the more remarkable in the instance of Hungary at the far eastern side of the Western European world, with the absolute governments of Turkey and Russia just yonder, and nearer the absolutism of Germany, the dominant Central European power. When we see fluctuations in the constitutional development of Hungary we get the significance of the Golden Bull. The lack of all constitutional safeguards for freedom in neighboring states in 1222 makes it glow like a beacon burning on a mountain top at night.

Churches are houses of hope, some speaking confusedly and others more clearly, but all interpreting according to their ability. Constitutional capitols and courts of law are houses of order, speaking clearly or confusedly according to their development, all on their way to give better service according as we advance in civilization. Just as there is real kinship in spirit between all liberty loving peoples, so there is a potential friendship and common concern between constitutional governments. The Magna Cartas and Golden Bulls of the world are expressions of one and the same spirit, and speak the common language of freedom. To this great association of the sons of liberty Hungary belongs of right. So especially does Transylvania. The Golden Bull sprang from the Magyars of Transylvania. If we would have a constitutionally governed international world, constitutionally minded peoples must see to it at the Peace tables that constitutional government shall continue for all Transylvania, Roumanians, Magyars, Saxons, and the others. The peace and prosperity of Transylvania must not be jeopardized by either the passions of irredentism or the fading forms of Byzantine tyranny.

VI

LOUIS KOSSUTH

THE FIGURE of Arpad sits astride his bronze horse in Buda-pest. Remarkable, is it not, that people have cared and remembered him for a thousand years? Kossuth, Arpad's successor long after, has many statues, and one of them stands on the Riverside Drive in New York, put there some seventy-five years after his memorable visit to this country. Remarkable, is it not, that Americans of Magyar descent and other American citizens have remembered Louis Kos-suth so long and cared for him so deeply that they placed his statue in the New York Park to stand there we hope for another thousand years?

Except for Lafayette, who had identified himself with us in our struggle for national independence, no foreign visitor to the United States up to the time of his coming ever had received such a welcome as was given to Kossuth in 1851. He never had touched our national history or our affairs. We owed him no debt of gratitude as we did Lafayette; but he had fought for freedom, and had become the embodiment of what this country stood for and stands for. And now, a little more than seventy-five years after his stay of a few months with us, his statue on Morningside Drive was being unveiled. Five hundred of his countrymen had come from

Hungary to honor the occasion, hundreds more of them had journeyed from all parts of this country and Canada, thousands of other men and women marched up New York's Fifth Avenue, and more thousands stood cheering along the way.

A curious incident occurred, symbolic of Kossuth's fame and teachings. A strong wind was blowing in off the sea. Overhead an aircraft dropped pamphlets impertinent to the occasion concerning some labor dispute; the agency conducting this surprising demonstration was not American. Hundreds of the leaflets fluttered downward, and then continuously the wind surging between the high buildings caught them, and carried them upward and away. Few reached the ground. And the great voice of Nicholas Jozan could be heard shouting, "See how the winds of God fight for us!"*

Here indeed was drama. Louis Kossuth, advocate of liberty under law, of constitutionality, Regent of Hungary, defeated by Austria but only by the help of Russian armies, a man without a country, an exile, but feted in Britain and the United States as few men have ever been; and now decades after his death he was symbolically marching up Fifth Avenue on this March morning in 1928, and was being given another tremendous welcome in the city where he had been so welcomed long before. Then it had taken a whole day for his procession to pass the reviewing stand. Still he speaks! Still he works for freedom! Still he begs the nations to federate for their common good, and the winds of God blow his teachings to the ends of the earth!

* Unitarian Bishop of Transylvania. On this occasion sent to the United States to represent the Hungarian Senate, of which he was then a member.

He was born at Monok, Northern Hungary, in 1802, graduated with honors at the College of Saros-Patak when seventeen years of age, and began the study of law at Eperjes. Finishing at Pest, he returned to Monok and although but twenty years old was made Honorary Attorney for the County, a position resembling that of District Attorney in the United States.

Later in life he was to become a famous public speaker, "eloquent," "impassioned," and he early began to use this talent. Angered at the Hapsburg complete disregard of the Hungarian constitution, and the suffering the tyranny caused, he vigorously protested, speaking wherever opportunity offered. Then a public calamity put him forward. Asiatic cholera struck the land with terrible force. Men died at the plough and in the streets; thousands fled the country. Terror drove men mad, and in a sort of delirium it was rumored that the upper people were poisoning the wells. Mobs began to attack them. Kossuth was everywhere, speaking, reasoning, persuading, starting relief work in which great numbers joined him. Soon he was welcomed in cottage and palace, and public gratitude took form.

It happened that a magnate was absent from the Diet. Kossuth was chosen to fill his place temporarily, and served 1825-27. By rights his position was more titular than active, as he had no vote; soon, however, he was called on to speak, and his eloquence and deep conviction at once made him a power. Such was the beginning of his long political career.

The times were hard. Throughout the land there was great bitterness and strife. Kossuth was appalled by the people's ignorance about what was happening in the national Diet. He learned shorthand, took down the more notable speeches and tried to publish them, but he found that an ancient law forbade their printing. Next he had the speeches lithographed, against which there was no law; but as the Austrian Government turned them aside in the post-offices they did not reach their destinations. Then he did something new. Volunteer secretaries copied the speeches in longhand, and delivered them to key people all over the country. Some of these handwritten reports reached editions of ten thousand copies, and provoked a tremendous response. There were many repercussions and Kossuth became a marked man. Throughout this period Transylvania was constantly and worthily represented in the conflicts.

We must restrict ourselves in this brief review to looking at the pattern of events, rather than at the events themselves, for the historical movements we are so briefly tracing were most intricate and varied. The Magyars, particularly those in Transylvania, stand out boldly. "Of the nationalities in the Austrian Monarchy," says Mr. Taylor, "only one had a completely genuine, unspoilt, and ingrained national tradition—the Magyars: even when most of Hungary had been in the hands of the Turks, the (Transylvanian) Diet at Pressburg had kept the tradition alive, and the Hapsburg attacks on Hungarian privileges had never lasted long enough to interrupt it. Moreover, the Magyar nobility had the inestimable advantage of possessing, in the central plain of Hungary a Magyar peasantry, so that the defense of privilege could be transformed into a struggle for national emancipation. And because Magyar nationalism already existed and did not have to be re-created, the Magyars—and the Magyars alone—got what they wanted in the nineteenth century, and by the end of it were dominant not merely in Hungary (where they were in a minority) but in many ways throughout the Empire." *

As we study these decades thousands of people seem to hurry to and fro before us. In Pozsony, now Bratislava, where the Hungarian Diet was sitting, in Buda and Pest, yonder in Vienna, in other parts of the Empire as well as throughout Hungary, there was a passionate surge of the people toward freedom and like a high cliff against which it vainly dashed itself stood the might of absolutism, an all controlling implemented tyranny. In this interplay of forces, with dungeon, scaffold, and imperial armies, great men cry out and disappear. Above them all looms Kossuth, a man of the people, fighting for freedom, his voice the voice of Hungary heard around the world.

Before we briefly study the events which made him one of the most revered and beloved of men, we must remember that the Austrians were not constitutionalists and that the Hungarians were. Unrest under Hapsburg tyranny in the other states comprising the Empire was by no means unknown, but it did not reveal the extraordinary constitutional mindedness of the Magyars.

Many books might be written on this single aspect of Magyar character, but two illustrations must suffice. During the century and a half of Turkish occupation more than a half of the Hungarians were held by the invader, while the nobles formerly living among them were scattered in the uninhabited parts. The peasants paid taxes to their absent landlords as well as to the Turks. Our second illustration shows the same spirit. The counties were then the ad-

* "The Austrian Monarchy," J. A. P. Taylor, Fellow of Magdalene College, Oxford. London, 1942, p. 79.

ministrative units, and among the exiled were the former county officials. During the entire period, while there were no county duties to be performed the exiled members of each county council met twice a year, filled the accurring vacancies in their ranks by regular elections, and continued at least the form of their autonomous life and institutions. When at last after a century and a half the Turkish occupation ended these men returned to their home counties, and the county councils at once began to function. It would be hard to find equals to the many illustrations of the Magyar constitutional mindedness.

"The Hapsburgs had no reason for valuing Magyar nationality higher than German or Slavonic," says Macartney, "while the strong Magyar spirit of loyalty was to them the very embodiment of truculent rebellion. The Hapsburgs waged a long war against this spirit, by methods which ranged from massacre to flattery. Some went out against the Magyars with fire and sword, some forced the Protestants by terror and persecution back into the Catholic fold; some enticed the high nobility to Vienna, loaded them with favors, and estranged them from their people. By one or another means, they managed to reduce very greatly both those liberties and the will to defend them."*

Such were the conditions Kossuth faced. In all that followed he was fighting the fight of free men everywhere. His fight was a part of the war of the United Nations for freedom. He was struggling for liberty under law, for constitutionality, upheld by Hungary for centuries, upheld by Transylvania alone when Hungary lay low under the Turks, denied and abhorred by Austria. Kossuth, leader of the Magyars, becomes a leader of free men everywhere.

* Macartney, "Hungary and Her Successors," p. 9.

"All Kossuth wanted," says Zarek, "was a free Hungary, free from the tutelage of Austria, free from the illegal interference of the Vienna central government in the rights of Hungary that were guaranteed her by her ancient constitution." And all this becomes obvious when we read Kossuth's demands.*

The coup d'etat of Napoleon III, by which he seized France, was giving face to absolutism everywhere. The tide of constitutionality, of guaranteed freedom, had appeared to be coming in, now was it receding? "There is a tide in the affairs of men." If ever the Magyars were to get their constitutional rights Kossuth and his followers felt that now was the time, they could not wait. The issue was joined. The Emperor, lord of vast domains, forgot that in Hungary he was only a constitutional king, bound to observe the rights of his people. To Austria Hungary was a province, its constitution no more than window dressing. Austria wanted Hungarian wealth. Ore from the ancient Transylvanian goldmines went straight to Vienna.† Industries were always discouraged and frequently hindered. Hungary was expected to supply Austria with raw materials, and buy back manufactured articles at more than it would have cost her to make them. Hungary was to do only as she was told with her own affairs, never was she freely to develop. And meanwhile Hungary talked to Austria about the constitutional partnership of equals!

On the fourth of March, two days after the news of the French Revolution of February, 1840, reached Pozsony, where the Hungarian Diet was sitting, Kossuth spoke dan-

* Printed at the end of this chapter.
† Until gold began to be brought in from America the Transylvanian mines were a chief source. Worked from Roman times, they are still in use.

gerously, "My mind is clouded with almost the grief of despair. The curse of a stifling vapor weighs upon us—a pestilential air sweeps over our country from the charnel-house of the Vienna Council of State, sapping our power, and exerting a deadening effect upon our national spirit. Hitherto my anxiety has been caused ... by seeing the constitutional progress of our (Hungarian) nation unsecure, and by seeing how the antagonism that has existed for three centuries between the absolutist government of Vienna, and the constitutional tendency of the Hungarian nation, has not up to this day been reconciled, nor ever can be reconciled without the abandonment of either one or the other." (p. 73) He proposed that an address be presented to the throne asking for reforms. His speech foreshadowed a revolution. In Hungary the die was cast, either absolutism or constitutionality must go.

The whole contest is still so much a part of our world situation a century after that we must get the black and white contrasts. On the one hand the Emperor as constitutional king of Hungary could not consistently ignore the Hungarian constitution; but if he desired he could, on the other hand, grant the same right claimed by Hungary to all his other dominions, and become a constitutional emperor.* This is precisely what Kossuth wanted.

The Hungarian complaint among other matters concerned the Vienna Council of State, which opposed the Hungarian Diet's constitutional policies and was deaf to its pleas. The Diet demanded its own Hungarian Cabinet back again. "For six hundred years," Kossuth told the Diet, "we formed a constitutional state. We resolve therefore from this moment that ministers again sit upon these benches to

* See Daniel Webster's comment, Chapter IX, p. 84.

hear and answer our questions." It was a daring and provocative proclamation.

The address to the Emperor was duly voted, Kossuth was made a member of the commission to present it, and became the spokesman. Consider what the two men about to face each other stood for. Kossuth was the personification of a tenacious, stubbornly constitutional people. From the earliest days they had elected their kings. Inheritance of the throne within the dynasty had been almost unbroken; the Arpad dynasty continued for three hundred years, the Hapsburg and Hapsburg Lorraine for just under four centuries. Yet even such an heir as the Emperor himself had to be accepted and crowned by the nation before he could exercise his kingly privileges. Nor was this all, before he could be crowned he had to take the coronation oath. By the most solemn royal pledges that could be devised the Emperor and his predecessors, as kings of Hungary, had been obliged to swear before Almighty God to maintain peace and justice, protect the Church, punish evildoers, afford aid to the orphans and widows, *judge justly according to the laws of the land,* defend the country and its *rights,* and reconquer the dismembered parts of Hungary.*† These grim royal promises have been preserved in the coronation oaths of all Hungarian Kings from 1290 down, together with the coronation ceremonies of Andrew III. Joseph II, brother of poor Marie Antoinette, avoided his Hungarian coronation just because of its binding constitutional limitations. The Hungarians have proved themselves stolid consistent constitutionalists, and so have made a rich contribution to the world's constitutional record. Over against them

* Otto Zarek, History of Hungary, p. 76.
† Italics the author's.

stood the German conception of the Emperor, and abso-lutism. Said Kossuth, "Two crowns, constitutional and des-potic, cannot be worn by the same head, any more than a man can be good and evil at the same time."

This gives meaning to the scene between the Emperor and Kossuth. It is high drama, but the roles are confused. The absolutist Emperor hears Kossuth pleading for gov-ernment in Hungary by and for the people, demanding gov-ernment by law according to the Hungarian constitution, as had been the Hungarian way broken now and again but heroically maintained. The Emperor represents all the ab-solutists from Hitler back to the first savage chief. Kossuth represents you and me, plain folk determined to govern ourselves, millions and millions of us the whole world over.

These many millions of us hate the whole absolutist sys-tem. The United Nations fought it. But with all this said what a job the Emperor had! The very center of intrigue and combat, of course he did the things emperors would do. Men cast for speaking parts must say their lines! Take the presidents of our American colleges as a mild illustration. Any morning you can hear them calling through our finan-cial forests. All of them make the same noises when begging for money. May they find big heaps of it! So the emperors used to make the same noises when harassed by men like Kossuth. Aloud, "Yes, yes, my child; yes, yes!" Aside, "May the devil fly away with you: I'll help him!" Never was any coronation oath strong enough to prevent an em-peror from saying one thing and doing another.

Kossuth's delegation wanted an Hungarian Cabinet; the Emperor agreed. He agreed to everything that was asked, while an angry mob milled around the palace, and he swore big royal oaths that he would keep his royal promises, and the royal family and high government officials swore also. Having made this compact the Emperor, regardless of human woe, proceeded to stir up the peoples around Hungary to attack her, persuading them by arguments and gold, the Croats and Serbians, the Wallachs, Wends and Saxons. These people rose in bloody insurrection against the Magyars, sparing no age or condition, and in some places the attacks were marked by atrocities. In the southern provinces especially there was great suffering. A new constitution was issued at Olmutz, wiping out the last traces of the constitution of St. Stephen. The Emperor also tried, though not so successfully, to set the races within Hungary to fighting among themselves. He made and broke compacts, gave writings and cancelled them. In the whole dark chapter of calamities the Court, together with the whole absolutist regime it represented, feared not only Hungary but all of Europe, for absolutist affairs were not going too well. The Emperor risked war rather than compromise with constitutionalism, for he knew that it would be the beginning of the end of his absolutist rule.

While the Emperor was stirring up war against Hungary, planning his best to bedevil Kossuth and all who stood with him, the Hungarian Diet was waiting for the Emperor to begin keeping his promises, and even hoping that constitutional government might be given to all Austria. Kossuth told the Diet, "The proper and holy mission of our country (Hungary), as the oldest member of the (Austrian) Empire, and possessing a constitutional government, is to raise its voice in behalf of those sister nations under the same ruler. We would not ask for freedom for ourselves alone."*

Events moved quickly. There was an Austrian Revolu-

* Zarek, p. 76.

tion (1848), influenced by Kossuth, which was suppressed. Metternich's policy with Hungary had been to preserve Austrian ascendancy by kindling jealousies among her peoples. As has been said, the Emperor now went further and stirred up enmity toward Hungary among the neighboring nations. Under such conditions of course the Emperor could not begin his promised reforms! In 1836 he dissolved the Hungarian Diet, and while there was no Diet was a good time to get rid of troublemakers.

So in 1837 Kossuth, Wesselenyi, and others were arrested. Kossuth was "captured" while walking alone in a Budapest park, set upon and carried off to prison. There was no legal procedure. Without trial these leaders were condemned to a year of solitary confinement, at the end of it they were tried and sentenced for three years more. During the first year of imprisonment no reading or writing had been allowed.* For the longer term Kossuth was permitted to choose three books, but nothing political. He chose Shakespeare, an English grammar and Walker's dictionary. It took him a fortnight to understand the first page of "The Tempest." He already knew Hungarian, Slovak, Latin, German, French and Italian. Now he learned English. Later he was to astonish Britain and America by his Shakespearean vocabulary.

Events forced Austria in 1839 to allow the Hungarian Diet to reassemble, and it promptly made itself heard on the prisoners' behalf. It effectively refused to pass all government measures. Danger of war in 1840 forced Austria to moderate her decision, and Metternich gave way. The prisoners were freed, and Kossuth emerged from his con-

* For an account of Austrian treatment, see "My Prisons" by Silvio Pellico, author of Francesca da Rimini.

finement ill but not permanently broken. His aged master Wesselenyi had become blind, another colleague imprisoned at the same time had gone mad, and three others were dying of disease.

It was at this period, immediately after his liberation, that he married Theresa Meszlenyi, to his lasting happiness.

We recall one of his great contemporaries, Count Szechenyi, a man of high privilege and devoted public spirit, who warned Kossuth that his reforms would lead to war. He demanded the abolition of feudal burdens, including entailment on property, which bore so heavily on the people. Kossuth called Szechenyi "the greatest Hungarian."

"Was Kossuth really the hero of the Magyar nation, as his people think him today?" asks Otto Zarek. "Or was he rather Hungary's prophet, the poet of a new future for this isolated, strongly individual and favored nation?" He was both.

How terrific are history's might have beens! Hungary was beating Austria. If only she could have finished it! If only a liberated Austria could have become a constitutional empire, and spreading in Central Europe had become the Danubian Federation we dream of today, if only Kossuth's plans had succeeded the lives of millions of free men killed in the two world wars would have been saved.

Was Hungary really winning in the war with Austria? The proof is that the Austrian Emperor begged help from Russia, and that the Czar promptly marched 130,000 trained and well equipped soldiers into Hungary.* General Görgey, whom Kossuth had appointed, overwhelmed by numbers was forced to surrender. So Hungary paid for try-

* Estimates differ. Another authority says, "Czar Nicholas sent an army of 250,000." Heroes of Hungary, p. 62.

ing to keep her constitutional government and to extend freedom.

Kossuth fled to Turkey with a band of his followers. In the flight he carried a mysterious chest which he guarded jealously. On their last night in Hungary he rowed over the river unaccompanied to a lonely spot where beneath a great tree near the bank he buried his package. It was the Holy Crown of St. Stephen. Discovered two years later it was carried to Budapest. It was taken thence long after by the Germans.

Kossuth rowed back across the river to his companions, he knelt and kissed the ground. The following brief summary of what he said was given later by those who knelt with him.

"Forgive me, Hungary, forgive me who am now condemned to wander far from here because I strove for your welfare. Forgive me who can no longer call anything free save this little strip of soil where I now kneel with a handful of your loyal sons. Forgive me that so many of your sons have shed their blood for you because of me. I wanted a free nation, enjoying a freedom that only God can give. My principles were those of George Washington. I love you, Europe's most loyal nation."

"I wanted a free nation," said Kossuth. "My principles were those of George Washington." Said Daniel Webster, "The prevalence on the European continent of sentiments favorable to republican liberty is the result of the reaction of America on Europe."

Orators must use the flitting moment, be clear and brief and dramatic; we would not criticise. But the cold fact is that Webster claimed far too much. He forgot for the moment that the French Revolution had been an explosion of

liberal ideas which went soaring over the world; he ignored
the Golden Bull, the basis and the symbol of Magyar constitutionality through centuries, he failed to mention the
never ending fight of the Magyars for their own liberty, and
the thousand other expressions of the European will to freedom. He might more fairly have said that the Magyars were
fighting for those same freedoms, guaranteed them by their
ancient constitution, which only seventy years earlier we
Americans had established for ourselves in the United
States by our national independence.

How modest, and if we may venture the comment, how
American Kossuth's demands on Austria appear to us,—

An independent Hungarian ministry.

Abolition of censorship.

The Hungarian Diet to be established at Budapest.

Equality before the law for all men.

Removal of all foreign soldiers and their replacement by
Hungarian troops who should be sworn to support the
Hungarian Constitution.

Formation of a National Guard.

All political prisoners to be released. (Remember Kossuth's
four years in solitary confinement.)

Educational liberty.

Trial by jury.

Dissolution of the Vienna Court Chancellery, which really
governed all Hungary, and its power henceforth to vest
in the Hungarian Diet.

The union of Transylvania with Hungary. After the Turks
were expelled and Transylvanian independence ceased
Austria had governed the principality as a province of
the empire having no connection with Hungary.

VII

KOSSUTH'S AMERICAN VISIT
AND AFTERWARD

IN THE last half of the eighteenth century Britain was attempting to make the American colonies subservient to her trade and industries, somewhat as Austria later and far more thoroughly made Hungary subservient under her absolute government, a province instead of a constitutional partner. Washington fought to be rid of all British interference. Up to this point we remember his "principles," which Kossuth claimed as his.

Often we forget that Washington was also welding thirteen individualistic little states, only slightly related, into a nation. E Pluribus Unum! One out of many! It was uphill work. "Who will deal with us," he cried, "when we are one nation today and thirteen tomorrow?" In the welter of their war it was the mutual concernments of these American Colonies, even despite themselves, that drew them haltingly together into a working whole, and made them a nation. Washington's principles were to make them one nation and to make them free.

When Kossuth knelt in farewell to Hungary he had been fighting to make her free, and also he had tried to extend

66

her constitutional liberties to the other states within the Austrian Empire. Later he wanted the countries around Hungary to federate for freedom and mutual protection. Whether he was aware of this larger inclusive purpose when he knelt in the dark by the river we do not know. But later he wanted federation. Perhaps his journeying through the States of our Union may have encouraged him. The dominant fact is that Kossuth adopted Washington's faith both in independence and federation.

The Sultan denied Kossuth's wish to proceed with his followers to Constantinople, but allowed him to stop in Asia Minor, first at Vidin, then at Shumla, and last at Kutaiah, giving him a handsome allowance on which he lived in some dignity as the President of Hungary. Austria hoped that he would now become as helpless as Napoleon had been at St. Helena. But isolated though he was for the next two years he still managed to keep up his fight for the liberation of Hungary. Subsequent events were no doubt due largely to his own persistent activity in exile.

As in every period of his life this banishment was full of color and unexpected action. He sent foreign agents about Europe, he had several of them, and he conducted an enormous correspondence in four languages reaching almost literally to the ends of the earth, making use of Hungarian, German, French and English. "A war of letters began," says Zarek, "a war without a parallel. Letters broadcast to the world, letters moving, provocating, argumentative." He could not believe that the free powers, he included the United States, would stand idly by and let Hungary be doomed to Austrian tyranny without striking a blow on her behalf. Was she not one of them, a free and constitutionally minded nation? Surely Britain and France and the United States could not fail to understand that Hungary's cause was theirs!

If these narrations seem far removed from Kossuth's visit to the United States, we must remember that our American interest in him was in no small part a reflection of Europe's concern. By the states around Hungary he was regarded as a possible ally; who indeed could tell but he might yet succeed? In France Napoleon III both feared and sought him. In England Lord Palmerston, nicknamed Lord Firebrand, then British Foreign Minister in Russell's cabinet, openly befriended him, although holding Austria to be "a European necessity and the natural ally of England in the East."* A Kossuth group formed in the British Parliament, including Richard Cobden and Lord Nugent together with other important members of the House. "It was possible," says Zarek, "that in England the fate of Hungary might yet be decided."†

Meantime Kossuth spent his days and much of his nights writing and writing his letters. For exercise he rode spirited horses. Considering his isolation his knowledge of current events was extraordinary. For example Pan-Slavism, and his comment on it has by some historians been called the beginning of the League of Nations. Said Kossuth, "The idea of Pan-Slavism can only be countered by the idea of federalism, that federation which guarantees small nations against foreign domination. This idea must and will prevail, most of all in Eastern Europe. For federation means liberty, Pan-Slavism slavery."† Kossuth was saying, fed-

* Kossary, History of Hungary, p. 243.
† Ibid., p. 242.

eration means liberty, dominance by one power means slavery; it is true to-day, especially in Transylvania.

In his exile he had not, as Austria hoped, retired into obscurity. On the contrary, more than ever before, he was now in the limelight. Even living in Asia Minor he was the very center of international interest. "Since Napoleon no name except Napoleon's was so known in the East." The world over men regarded him as a Martyr to Freedom. Austria came to believe that he was more dangerous in exile than he had been in Budapest, and she tried to get rid of him in several ways, including assassination, but the plot was discovered. Then she and Russia together demanded that the Sultan deliver him to them. Britain openly opposed their efforts and even suggestively sent a fleet of fourteen battleships to cruise along the Turkish shores. On the Sultan's refusal to deliver Kossuth to them Austria ended diplomatic relations with Turkey. It looked for a time as if the famous exile might yet cause war.

If these happenings were not so serious in their implications, the cause of freedom and death for Kossuth and others hanging in the balance, some of the events would take on an amusing appearance. For example, Kossuth issued a formal "proclamation to the free people of the United States of North America." We Americans received it gravely, read and commented on it all over the country, and praised it lavishly. It seemed no more incongruous then for Kossuth, the exiled President of Hungary, to address this country than it would recently have been for Mr. Churchill from his high office to address us. Probably this address precipitated, and partly caused the answer sent by the United States. The Senate unanimously offered Kossuth and his companions in exile an asylum here, and sent a battleship to Asia Minor to bring them hither.* Far from pleased with our interest in Kossuth, Austria protested. In his defense Daniel Webster, then Secretary of State, went to surprising lengths.† Webster was then seventy-one years old and nearing the end of his career. His biographers may yet decide that championing Kossuth was one of his most praiseworthy deeds. Before Kossuth could leave Turkey he had to receive the Sultan's permission, and no doubt Webster's influence counted.

History records many humorous situations. The Sultan is reported to have been little pleased to have Kossuth flee to Turkey, and after his arrival Kossuth had not settled down into obscurity. On the contrary men from all parts of the world kept coming to see him, and he kept on writing troublesome letters. Austria and Russia had been hammering at the Sultan's gate to get him, and failing they were now trying to make an arrangement with the Sublime Porte to detain him for at least five years, until Hungary should become pacified and his influence had burned out. And there were those fourteen British battleships sailing about the Dardanelles within his view. To the Sultan it must have been welcome news indeed when he learned that the United States had offered the exile and his companions a safe retreat where it was expected that they would remain for the rest of their lives. He gave them permission to depart, and he must have been well pleased when finally they went.

So the American battleship *Mississippi* which had been

* Senator Foote of Mississippi had made the motion in the Senate on Kossuth's behalf, and the selection of the ship *Mississippi* may well have been a courtesy to that State. The plan for Kossuth's relief was considered here as representing the whole nation.

† See Webster's letter to the Austrian representative, Chap. IX.

cruising back and forth off the Turkish shore while waiting sailed away with Kossuth, his wife and children, and some forty followers. The ship flew the American and Hungarian flags. The commander had received Kossuth as the President of Hungary, which as far as it went was an American recognition of his claims.

Who can blame Kossuth if he believed that these many attentions promised help in another war against Austria! For a time England seemed about to aid him,* if not with arms then with diplomacy. But the United States, lavish as we were with our welcome, never dreamed of sending American armies to Eastern Europe. We were glad to praise Kossuth, we would advise Europe, certainly; giving Europe advice has long been one of our favorite national pastimes. But as for fighting Austria it never entered our provincial heads! It took us a century after Kossuth's day to become internationally minded; even in the Air Age with distances abolished it proved a slow development. We are not suggesting that the United States should have gone to war with Austria on Hungary's behalf. At the time it would have been geographically impossible, the mere suggestion is quixotic; but in his desperate earnestness for his beloved Hungary how human it was for Kossuth to hope for help both from Britain and the United States.

The Italian governments would not permit Kossuth to land on his way here, nor would France, no nation was asking for trouble with Austria; but there were heartwarming

---

* Britain "did not hesitate to support oppositional moves against Austria when, stricken by domineering obstinacy, she refused to make her numerous peoples equal members of a commonwealth, throwing over them all the shame of a short-sighted absolutism." Statement by F. Milkin Hodža, former Prime Minister of Czechoslovakia, "Federation in Central Europe," p. 163.

demonstrations, cheering crowds along the shores and bonfires on the hills. At Marseilles Jean Jonquil plunged naked
into the sea and swam a long way out to the battleship.
When Kossuth asked him how he could swim so far he answered, "Where there is the will nothing is impossible," and
Kossuth ever after used the phrase as his slogan. Jonquil
was not his only visitor, thousands of Marseilles visited
him aboard the ship. He addressed himself to the working
people of France in a newspaper article, announcing his
sympathy with them. The social struggle was about to
begin. "The stop at Marseilles," says Zarek, "was of great
political significance. In the coming struggle the workers
of France could cite Kossuth as their spiritual leader."*

At last he reached England. It is not within our scope to
tell of his English visit, beyond saying that few men ever
had been so welcomed. Crowds went to London to see him.
He was given the use of the Lord Mayor's coach. He was
wined and dined and shown all possible attention everywhere he went; he was made to travel and speak and receive delegations. The *Mississippi* had preceded him to
this country with most of his companions, and after a short
stay he took ship again and followed them.

Except Lafayette, let it be repeated, no visitor to the
United States had ever received such a welcome. Memorial
coins were issued, one side carried his appeal for freedom
and the other side, "Louis Kossuth, the Washington of
Hungary." He addressed Congress which no foreigner except Lafayette had ever been asked to do before. Kossuth
clubs sprang up everywhere and some of them continued in
1945; everywhere the red, white, and green colors of Hungary festooned the buildings and flew on our flagpoles with

* Kossuth, a Biography, Otto Zarek, p. 252.

the stars and stripes. Thousands of men wore the famous Kossuth hats, and the women wore red and white flowers which with the green leaves made the Hungarian colors, and they carried bouquets of them. As Kossuth journeyed the country gave itself up to festival, and far beyond his strength he shook thousands of hands, attended endless banquets, and made five hundred speeches in the seven months of his stay, each about one hour long, an average of thirteen a week. The nationwide scope of his travels and the tremendous enthusiasm with which he was received are amazing.

"He is here," wrote Horace Greeley, "to arouse us to the majesty of our national position, and to show us that we cannot safely sleep while despots are forging chains for the yet unfettered nations; that we must assume resistance to the expanding dominion of the Autocrat if only to secure our own. The free nations cannot afford to leave each other to be assailed in succession, and overwhelmed and crushed. May he leave our shores strengthened by substantial aid." (Abbreviated) Greeley hopes that Americans "will give or lend" a few million dollars "to free Hungary, and thereby insure the speedy emancipation of all Europe." But Greeley does not suggest that we send armies to help Kossuth, only dollars. Europe in 1851 was psychologically a long way off, and Hungary was on the other side of the world.

Such were the sentiments Kossuth heard expressed as he went about the country, westward to the Mississippi, there was then little beyond it, south to New Orleans, back again along the Atlantic seaboard to New York. Shoutings and bonfires, processions and banquets, and not a little money flowing in for the cause,* no penny of which Kossuth would

* In all about $100,000.

touch for himself. Quantities of old guns and pistols, antiquated and useless, were given him; what became of them is not clear.

"You have got your story told in every palace and log hut and prairie camp throughout this country," Ralph Waldo Emerson told him in a public welcome given him in Concord, Massachusetts, two months before he was to leave, May 11, 1852. And the story Kossuth told has been remembered ever since. Some seventy years later Masaryk* writes during the First World War how he observed that Kossuth's memory in the United States as a champion of freedom and democracy was still a living reality.

Emerson continued in his welcome, "As the shores of Europe and America approach every month, and their politics will one day mingle, when the crisis arrives it will find us all instructed beforehand in the rights and wrongs of Hungary, and parties already to her freedom. . . . You have achieved your right to interpret our Washington." Emerson had just described Kossuth as "a man so truly in love with the greatest future, that he cannot be diverted to anything less." He also had said, "We knew beforehand that you would not go by us in Concord. . . . Therefore we sat and waited for you." All this to be sure was honorable speech for a great philosopher, whose works gathered in twelve stout volumes are read by thousands of people in all the world's great languages.

But Kossuth, man of action, wearied to the bone, was fighting for Hungary's freedom with all the life there was in him, with complete devotion and enthusiasm.† There

* In his World Revolution.
† "Whoever condemns enthusiasm," said Kossuth. "tears up man's patent of nobility." Zarek, p. 161.

was altogether too much of this sitting about and waiting, and he answered Emerson with a notable prophecy. "There was never yet a more fatal mistake," he told the Concord Assembly, "than it would be to believe that by not caring about the political condition of Europe, America may remain unaffected by it. Yes, gentlemen, either America will regenerate the condition of the Old World, or it will be degenerated by the condition of the Old World."

He was a true prophet. Sixty-two years later we learned it during the First World War in 1914. And we learned it again early in the Second World War ninety years afterward when Germany had been perfecting her plans for the invasion of the United States. The airlines in South America were in German hands, bases had been selected, conquest of the Panama Canal had been laid out minutely, demolition of American cities had been carefully determined on— as in Rotterdam; why not destroy American centers when they were easily reached by air and were quite unprotected? Regenerate Europe, said Kossuth, or be degenerated. And the end is not yet. In the spring of 1945 it was reported that the American State Department had received photostat copies of German plans for a third world war. Copies of the plans were said to have been sent to the state departments of all the other United Nations. When the next war comes, and whether or not it comes depends on the success of the United Nations in organizing world peace, remember that there is no guarantee whatever that we could win a third time. Emerson's detachment, ten years later he hardly realized that the Civil War was going on, must have been maddening to Kossuth. He was right!

What else could these American experiences have meant to him, we ask ourselves again, except that the United

States and Britain were about to help free Hungary? Not until it was all over, not until the shouting and the tumult had died, did poor Kossuth realize that while we had enjoyed seeing and hearing him, we never had had any intention of fighting. The situation is indeed not without its pathos!

Kossuth and his wife left New York quietly July 14, 1852, making their steamer reservations under an assumed name, slipping away almost as fugitives, for they really could not endure a formal farewell with all its fuss and fatigue. That they departed grateful for the many honors shown them cannot be doubted; but neither can we doubt that this great fighter for freedom left us in deep disappointment. In his very soul he had hoped that the free nations would help Hungary. For this end he had worked without respite, even in times of physical exhaustion and collapse which endangered his life. Britain and the United States had taken him to their hearts, but neither of them would go to war with Austria.

He lived for a time in England. He went to the continent, interviewing statesmen, and carrying on his endless letter writing. One of his efforts concerns us because it was of importance to Hungary and especially to Transylvania.

Roumania, or what is now that country, then consisted of two principalities, Moldavia and Wallachia, both under Turkish sovereignty. Alexander Couza, Prince of Moldavia, was elected also Prince of Wallachia with the union of the two principalities. It was planned to federate Hungary, Serbia, and perhaps Croatia. Here was a beginning of Danubian Federation. In the compact it was stipulated that it should be left to a Transylvanian congress whether Transylvania should be a part of Hungary or become autonomous. Precisely what we are pleading for in this book had won the approval of the contracting parties, and all seemed to be progressing happily toward its fulfillment, when precisely what has happened every time Danubian Federation is approached, happened here. Big powers stood in the way. Austria and Turkey objected. England supported Austria, while Russia and France with others powers approved. Kossuth spoke to great meetings in England, but without avail on the government.

It is only fair to remember on behalf of those who hesitated that black cloudbanks covered the political skies, a storm was brewing. While Central Europe appeared to be in a softened condition so that new political forms might be started with hope of success, some of the big powers were afraid to upset the status quo. The Crimean War was unfolding with all its involvements. Yet it is not without historical importance that before the storm broke Kossuth was helping on a Danubian Federation. Does not the plan for some form of federation among the Danubian states, always being turned aside yet recurring, suggest inevitability? Perhaps not this time, but the ship will float off the bar on the next highest tide when the moon is full! To his great credit Kossuth had again ridden into the tourney spear in place, and again he had been unhorsed. But the cause of autonomy for Transylvania remained and still remains persistent.

Kossuth in 1861 established himself in Italy, making his home in Turin, where he died in 1894, ninety-two years of age. To the end of his days by his writings he continued pleading for Hungary.

Most of his portraits are libels, in the worst style of the period happily now ended. The young Emperor Franz Joseph, for example, is presented in a famous portrait as a pleasing youth in uniform with a wasplike waist, no more than eighteen inches around, his broad shoulders tapering down to his tiny belt like the letter V. If ever he really appeared as this painting shows him he must have been stoutly corseted. Kossuth is often pictured wearing a high feathered hat, a cape thrown around him with studied carelessness, his hand on his sword or pressing his heart dramatically, his general air often being one of maidenly timidity. Even his "American portrait," with its fine head and face, depicts him with a robe thrown over one shoulder, holding a scroll and leaning against a pillar, a pose better fitted to Hamlet than to the leader of wars for freedom. Says Zarek, "He was handsome. All his portraits show a virile head, clearly the head of a clever, good, imaginative man." His last picture, done when he was about ninety, shows us a commanding face, with strength, high intelligence and even with beauty.*

Many American writers were as unkind to him as the portrait painters. "Kossuth's address," we read, "enchained the auditory; its only interludes were the waves of emotion that found utterance in the universal language of applause." Tons of such stuff were printed and read, but a century after it is hard to feel any glow. These fashions of the past have made Kossuth needlessly obscure. Nonetheless he stands before us today strong and vital when all the tyranny he hated and all the freedom he loved and served have clashed so mightily.

His writings are vibrant. In his "letter to the people of the United States" he tells us what he fought for. "I asked Austria first, for nothing more than a constitutional ministry (for Hungary); second, for a reform in the administration of the (Hungarian) State; and third, that the free-

* Now in the Danbelovsky Collection in Vienna.

dom granted Hungary be extended to the other nations in the Empire."

"The King and Royal family having given their royal oaths that these changes should be granted," he explains, "on the very day they signed these grants, and swore before God to maintain them, they secretly planned the most cruel conspiracy. They determined on insurrection, conflagration and blood until exhausted Hungary might be struck from the roll of living nations. They hoped by the bayonet, and if necessary by the arms of Russia, to erect an empire like the Russian of sixteen various nations, they hoped to make themselves an absolute power."

"I called the nation to arms in self defense."

Daniel Webster, then Secretary of State, well knew what principles the three countries—Austria and Russia against Hungary—stood for. His two famous statements, one has been given, are tremendously worth pondering. A year after the first he said at a public meeting and really addressing this country and Europe, "We have all had our sympathies much enlisted in the Hungarian effort for liberty. We have all wept at its failure. Despotic power (Russia) stepped in to suppress that hope.

"The Emperor of Russia demands of Turkey that the noble Kossuth and his companions shall be given up. There is something on earth greater than despotic power, and that is the aroused indignation of the whole civilized world. If the Emperor of Russia shall perpetrate so great a violation of national law as to seize these Hungarians and execute them, he will stand as a criminal in the view of the public law of the world. Let us consider the mission which Providence seems to have designed for us (Americans). May we stand up, and with a voice not to be disregarded, and say, 'This shall not be done, at least not without our protest!' "*

No American Secretary of State ever shouted louder into royal ears. His utterance is amazing, and it is equally amazing that the country supported him, applauded and approved.

We in the United States have long been interested in the entire Hungarian problem, of which Transylvania has brokenly been a part. Now, severed again from Hungary, her doom to be a province of Roumania, or—putting all thought of her becoming again a part of Hungary aside—to follow the will of her people and become autonomous will come before the Peace Conference. Maybe for the peace of the world you can help shape public opinion. Is it too much to beg for an autonomous Transylvania within a federation of Hungary and Roumania and neighboring states, so that succeeding generations shall not continue to be raised for cannon fodder? Shall the youth of these lands forever be driven to the shambles?

* Speech, 1851, published throughout the country.

VIII

KOSSUTH'S SISTERS IN AMERICA

THE THREE exiled sisters of Louis Kossuth fled to the United States in 1853, where two years before their brother had been welcomed; Mme. Susanne Meszlenyi, Mme. Emillia Zulavsky and Mme. Louise Ruttkay.

The story of their coming centers around the life and work of Mrs. Meszlenyi. It was she who urged Kossuth to start the Post Gazette, his great weapon for freedom, and helped him edit it. After the death of her husband in 1848 she became superintendent of hospitals in Hungary. After the war she was captured by the Austrians and imprisoned, but was released a year later. She then opened a boarding school and supported her own family, her sisters and their families. The Austrian Government, believing that she was doing propaganda work against Austria, closed the school in 1851 and she was again put in prison.

On the intervention of Queen Victoria she and her family were freed in 1853. They immediately set out to join Kossuth, who was then in London. On the way, Kossuth's mother died at Brussels. The Belgian Government, fearing the Hapsburgs, denied Kossuth entry into the country to attend his mother's funeral. Mrs. Meszlenyi died the following month after reaching America and was buried in the lot of the First Presbyterian Church, New York City. Her four sons served in the Union Army during the Civil War. Three of them gave their lives. Ladislas, the second son, rose to be a Colonel, and after the Civil War fought with Garabaldi in Italy.*

Mrs. Zulavsky, Kossuth's second sister, died in Brooklyn in 1860. She had made a wide circle of friends, among them Henry Wadsworth Longfellow, who wrote a poem about her which was read at the funeral. She was buried in Greenwood Cemetery in the section belonging to the Church of Our Saviour (Unitarian), of Brooklyn. Her stone bears this inscription, "Ye who return when Hungary is free, oh, take my dust along, my heart is there."

She wore on her wrist an iron chain, symbol of the chains that Austria had put on Hungary. Shortly before her death she was given a grapevine brought from the fatherland, packed in its native soil. She asked that some of the earth about its roots be put in her grave, which was done. A large grapevine is growing today nearby, no doubt the same vine. The iron chain lies buried with her; the vine still seeks the sunlight. The hope she cherished for Hungary's welfare like her vine is deep-rooted, it lives and grows.

Mrs. Ruttkay, the third sister, returned to Europe late in life to live with her brother, Louis Kossuth, in Turin, Italy. A fragment of a charming letter has survived, written by their niece, which gives us a comforting picture of the great leader. It is dated at Nice, December 27th, 1885: "On my way back from Hungary I remained three weeks in Turin

* In 1860 some 4000 Magyars lived in America. About 800 served in the Union Army of whom from 80 to 100 were officers. "Hungarians in America," Joseph C. Roucek, Hungarian Quarterly, Summer Edition, 1937, Vol. III, No. 2.

with Aunt Ruttkay and my dear Uncle Kossuth. He is the most beautiful, the most ideal of old men, and I learned to love him with all my heart and reverence him. He lives the life of a recluse, absorbed in his studies and writings, gaining thereby a comfortable income. I was glad to find aunt in such a pleasant and quiet harbor during her old age. She has delightful apartments, and a handsomely furnished little salon for her own special use; no responsibility or care but the mere supervision of her small household. Both of uncle's sons are living away from him now, their professional duties calling them elsewhere. I hear they are quite remarkable men, inheriting something of their father's intellect and character. I shall never forget those quiet evenings passed in Kossuth's study, where we always spent the hours between dinner and bedtime. Often he talked with me, recounting events in his past life, recalling incidents of that time when he was moving the hearts of the nations with the wonderful power of his eloquence,—an eloquence the magic of which I could well understand, listening to him. He was very kind and loving with me, and I feel that my whole life will be richer for having known and loved him. He carries his eighty-three years vigorously, walks four or five miles a day, and his intellect seems in no way dimmed by age. He reads and writes much of the time without glasses, and the old fire still possesses his soul."

IX

DANIEL WEBSTER TELLS AUSTRIA

DANIEL WEBSTER put the United States squarely behind Hungary in his famous rebuke to Austria. He reflected public opinion throughout the country, and as Secretary of State he was acting for the President. He writes,* "My letter (to Austria) is boastful and rough. I thought it well to speak out, and tell the people of Europe who and what we are." The United States, then small and distant, held no such looming vantage place in the world's perspective as she holds today. Europe for the most part disregarded her. Webster well knew that with Austria as a sounding board he would be heard over the world. He makes the United States the champion of constitutional liberty wherever it exists.

The might have beens! If Russia had not sent her 130,-000 well equipped soldiers against the poorly armed volunteers whom Kossuth miraculously had assembled, and who were beating the Austrians; if only the United States could have recognized the constitutional government of Hungary! Well, Webster's letter is worth the reading.

Here are the actors in the drama. President Taylor had

* Letter to Mr. Ticknor, January 16, 1851.

sent A. Dudley Mann to Austria as a confidential agent of the United States Government to observe the Hungarian Revolution. On receiving Mr. Mann's report the President submitted it to the Senate and it became public. The Austrian Charge d'Affaires at Washington, Chevalier J. G. Hülsemann, protested. What follows is only the pith of Mr. Webster's reply, shorn of diplomatic circumlocution and abbreviated. The words, however, are Mr. Webster's.*

"The object of Mr. Hülsemann's note are first, to protest against the steps taken by the late President (Taylor) to ascertain the progress and probable result of the revolutionary movements in Hungary and secondly, to complain of instructions given by the late Secretary of State to Mr. A. Dudley Mann, a confidential agent of the United States, and communicated to the Senate.

"The principal protest is that the United States by sending Mr. Mann has interfered in the domestic affairs of Austria. The President's message was a communication to the Senate transmitting (Mr. Mann's) correspondence. The Austrian Cabinet by the instructions given to Mr. Hülsemann was itself interfering with the domestic concerns of a foreign State.

"Had it been the pleasure of the Emperor of Austria (during the Hungarian struggles) to have admonished the 'provisional' (Hungarian) government, or the people of that country, against involving themselves in disaster by following the evil and dangerous example of the United States of America in making efforts for the establishment of independent governments, such admonition would not have originated here (in the United States) any diplomatic correspondence. And further, the President might have declined

* From Webster's "Great Speeches," Edwin R. Whipple.

to direct any particular reply to Mr. Hülsemann's note, but it has been thought better to answer that note at length upon the topics which it discusses.

"The leading subject in the note is the correspondence between Mr. Hülsemann and my predecessor in which (the last Secretary of State) informed Mr. Hülsemann that Mr. Mann's mission to Austria had no other object than to obtain reliable information as to the true state of affairs in Hungary. This (explanation) ought to be deemed quite satisfactory. Mr. Hülsemann (asserts that our reply) says little as to the cause of our anxiety to ascertain the chances of the Revolution.

"Justice to President Taylor's memory requires the present Secretary of State briefly to restate the history of these steps. The Emperor of Austria (surely) does not think that the Government of the United States ought to view with unconcern the extraordinary events which have occurred, not only in his dominions, but in many parts of Europe, since (the French Revolution of February, 1848). The Government and the people of the United States take a lively interest in the movements and events of this remarkable age, in whatever part of the world they may be exhibited; but this does not proceed from any disposition to depart from that neutrality toward foreign powers, which is among the deepest principles of the Union. In proportion as these extraordinary events appear to have their origin in those great ideas of responsibility on which the American constitutions are wholly founded, they could not but command the warm sympathy of the people of this country. Well known circumstances (in our history) have made (us) the representatives of popular principles of government: (the people of this country) cannot conceal their character, or their destiny. They cannot shut out from the view of mankind the causes which have placed them in the station they now hold. They cannot suppress the thoughts or hopes which arise in men's minds, in other countries, from contemplating their successful example of free government. The Emperor Joseph II was among the first to discern this necessary consequence of the reaction of the American Revolution on the opinions of (European) people. In a letter in 1787 (the Emperor) observes: 'It is remarkable that France, by the assistance which she afforded to the Americans, gave birth to reflections on freedom.' This fact is now admitted by intelligent powers all over the world. The prevalence (on the European continent) of sentiments favorable to republican liberty is the result of America on Europe, and the source of this reaction is in these United States.

"The position thus belonging to the United States is inseparable from their history, constitutional organization, and character, as the opposite position of the powers composing the European alliance is inseparable from the history and constitutional organization of the governments of those powers. The sovereigns who form that alliance not infrequently have felt it their right to interfere with the political movements of foreign states; and have denounced the popular ideas of the age in terms so comprehensive as to include the United States and all other democratic forms of government. One of the leading principles of the allied sovereigns is that all popular or constitutional rights are held (only) as indulgencies from crowned heads. His late Austrian Majesty, Francis I, is reported to have declared in an address to the Hungarian Diet, in 1820, that 'the whole world has become foolish and were in search of imaginary constitutions.' These declarations amount to nothing less than a denial of the lawfulness of the origin of the Government of the United States since it was established in consequence of a change which did not proceed from thrones. The United States heard these denunciations of fundamental principles without remonstrance. This was thirty years ago.

"The power of this republic is spread over a region, one of the richest on the globe, in comparison with which the possessions of the House of Hapsburg are but as a patch on the earth's surface. Its population will exceed that of the Austrian Empire within the period during which it may be hoped that Mr. Hülsemann may yet remain in the discharge of his duties. Its navigation and commerce are hardly exceeded by the oldest and most commercial nations. Its maritime means and power may be seen by Austria herself on all seas where she has ports, also in all other quarters of the globe. Life, liberty, property and all personal rights are amply secured to all citizens and protected by just and stable laws; and credit, public and private, is as well established as in any government of continental Europe and the country partakes in all the improvements and progress which distinguish the age. Certainly, the United States may be pardoned, even by those who profess adherence to the principles of absolute government, if they entertain an ardent affection for those popular forms of political organization which have so rapidly advanced their own prosperity and enabled them to bring their country to the notice, not to say the admiration, of the civilized world. Nevertheless the United States have abstained from interference with the political changes of Europe. However, they cannot fail to cherish always a lively interest in the efforts of nations struggling for institutions like their own. This sympathy is quite consistent with amicable relations with them all.

"The attention (of the late President Taylor) was first drawn to the state of things in Hungary by Mr. Stiles, Charge d'Affaires of the United States at Vienna. In the autumn of 1848 an application was made to him on behalf of Mr. Kossuth, formerly Minister of Finance for the Kingdom of Hungary, and at the time chief of the Revolutionary Government. His object was to obtain the good offices of Mr. Stiles with the Imperial Government with a view to the suspension of hostilities. The conduct of Mr. Stiles (was) viewed with satisfaction by the Imperial Government (and) was approved by that of the United States.

"In 1848 and '49 a considerable number of Hungarians came to the United States. The President was strongly urged to recognize the existence of (the Revolutionary Hungarian Government). In the manner in which (these applications were presented) there was nothing unusual nor anything unauthorized by the law of nations. It was only in the event that the (new) Hungarian government should appear, in the opinion of (our) agent (Mr. Mann), to be firm and stable, that the President proposed to recommend its recognition.

"Mr. Mann did not enter Hungary. He reported against the recognition of her independence because he found that she had been unable to set up a firm and stable government. Mr. Hülsemann will feel how little foundation there is for his remark that 'those who did not hesitate to (send) Mr. Dudley Mann should have borne in mind that they were exposing their emissary to be treated as a spy.' A spy is a person sent by one belligerent to gain secret information (about the other) to be used for hostile purposes. To give

this odious name to a confidential agent of a neutral power
sent for a purpose fully warranted by the law of nations is
to confound all just ideas; the President directs the Secretary of State to say to Mr. Hülsemann that the American
Government would regard such imputation upon it as distinctly offensive if it did not presume that the word used in
the original German was not of equivalent meaning with
'spy' in English. Had the Imperial Government of Austria
subjected Mr. Mann to the treatment of a spy, the Cabinet
of Vienna may be assured the spirit of this people would
have demanded immediate hostilities to be waged by the
utmost exertion of the Republic, military and naval.

"In respect to the honorary epithet bestowed (on Mr.
Kossuth) in (the President's) instructions to Mr. Mann,
Mr. Hülsemann will bear in mind that the Government of
the United States cannot justly be expected to withhold
from an individual an epithet of distinction of which a great
part of the world thinks him worthy merely because (his
own government) regards him as a rebel. While Washington was considered by the English Government as a rebel
chief, he was regarded by the continent of Europe as an
illustrious hero. It is believed that the Emperor Joseph II
habitually spoke in terms of respect and admiration of the
character of Washington. In 1781 the Courts of Russia and
Austria proposed a diplomatic congress of the belligerent
powers, to which the Commissioners of the United States
should be admitted.

"Mr. Hülsemann thinks that improper expressions were
introduced in regard to Russia but (the Secretary of State)
has no reason to suppose that Russia herself is of that opinion. The only observation made is that 'Russia has chosen
to assume an attitude of interference,' and her immense

preparations for invading and reducing the Hungarians to the rule of Austria, from which they desired to be released, gave so serious a character to the contest as to awaken the most painful solicitude in the minds of Americans. The Austrian Cabinet is unnecessarily susceptible in looking on language like this as a 'hostile demonstration.'

"It was addressed by the Government to its own agent and received publicity only through the communication of one department of the American Government to another. The comity of nations would hardly forbid its being addressed to the two Imperial Powers themselves. The relations of the United States (with Russia) have always been of the most friendly kind. The fact that Austria had a faithful ally in Russia cannot alter the real nature of the question between Austria and Hungary, nor in any way affect the neutral rights and duties of the Government of the United States, or the justifiable sympathies of the American people. It is easy to conceive that favor toward struggling Hungary would not be diminished but increased when the army of Austria was upheld by a power whose assistance proved to be overwhelmingly destruction of all (Hungarian) hopes.

"Mr. Hülsemann remarks that if the Government of the United States were to take an indirect part in the political movements of Europe, American policy would be exposed to acts of retaliation. (As to this) hypothetical retaliation, the Government and people of the United States are quite willing to take their chances. They have no fear of events of the nature alluded to by Mr. Hülsemann. It would be idle now to discuss those acts of retaliation which may possibly take place at some indefinite time hereafter. Mr. Hülsemann and the Cabinet of Vienna may rest assured that in the meantime nothing will deter the Government or the people of the United States from exercising the rights that belong to them as an independent nation and of forming and expressing their own opinions, freely and at all times, upon the political events which may transpire. Their own institutions stand upon the broadest principles of civil liberty; believing them to be eminently favorable to the prosperity of states, to be, in fact, the only principles of government which meet the demands of the present enlightened age.

"The President has perceived with great satisfaction that in the constitution recently introduced into the Austrian Empire many of these great principles are recognized and applied, and he cherishes a sincere wish that they may produce the same happy effects throughout his Majesty's extensive dominions that they have done in the United States.

"The undersigned begs to repeat to Mr. Hülsemann assurance of his high consideration."

(signed) Daniel Webster.

X

WEBSTER SPEAKS AGAIN

AT A PUBLIC meeting in 1850 Daniel Webster, Secretary of State, spoke on Kossuth's behalf, and his speech was printed in the newspapers throughout the United States and in Europe.

"We have all had our sympathies much enlisted in the Hungarian effort for liberty. We have all wept at its failure. We thought we saw a more rational hope of establishing free government in Hungary than in any other part of Europe, where the question has been in agitation within the last twelve months. But despotic power (Russia) from abroad intervened to suppress that hope.

"And, Gentlemen, what will come of it I do not know. For my part, at this moment, I feel more indignant at recent events connected with Hungary than at all those which passed in her struggle for liberty. I see that the Emperor of Russia demands of Turkey that the noble Kossuth and his companions shall be given up, to be dealt with at his pleasure. And I see that this demand is made in derision of the established law of nations. Gentlemen, there is something on earth greater than arbitrary or despotic power. The lightning has its power, and the whirlwind has its power, and the earthquake has its power, but there is something among

men more capable of shaking despotic thrones than lightning, whirlwind, or earthquake, and that is, the excited and
aroused indignation of the whole civilized world. Gentlemen, the Emperor of Russia holds himself to be bound by
the law of nations, from the fact that he negotiates with
civilized nations, and that he forms alliances and treaties
with them. He professes in fact to live in a civilized age, and
to govern an enlightened nation. I say, that if, under these
circumstances, he shall perpetrate so great a violation of
national law as to seize these Hungarians and to execute
them, he will stand as a criminal and malefactor in the view
of the public law of the world. The whole world will be the
tribunal to try him, and he must appear before it, and hold
up his hand, and plead, and abide its judgment.

"The Emperor of Russia is the supreme lawgiver in his
own country, and, for aught I know, the executor of that
law also. But, thanks be to God, he is not the supreme lawgiver or executor of national law, and every offense against
that is an offense against the rights of the civilized world.
If he breaks the law in the case of Turkey, or any other
case, the whole world has the right to call him out, and to
demand his punishment.

"Our rights as a nation, like those of other nations, are
held under the sanction of national law; a law which becomes more important from day to day; a law which none,
who profess to agree to it, are at liberty to violate. Nor let
him imagine, that mere force can subdue the general sentiment of mankind. It is much more likely to diffuse that
sentiment, and destroy the power which he most desires to
establish and secure.

"Gentlemen, the bones of poor John Wickliffe were dug
out of his grave seventy years after his death, and burnt for

his heresy; and his ashes were thrown upon a river in War-
wickshire. Some prophet of that day said:

'The Avon to the Severn runs
The Severn to the sea,
And Wickliffe's dust shall spread abroad
Wide as the waters be.'

"Gentlemen, if the blood of Kossuth is taken by an absolute, unqualified, unjustifiable violation of the national law,
what will it appease, what will it pacify? It will mingle with
the earth, it will mix with the waters of the ocean, the whole
civilized world will snuff it in the air, and it will return with
awful retribution on the heads of those violators of national
law and universal justice. I can not say when, or in what
form; but depend upon it, that, if such an act take place,
then thrones, and principalities, and powers, must look out
for the consequences.

"And now, Gentlemen, let us do our part; let us understand the position in which we stand, as the great republic
of the world, at the most interesting era of its history. Let
us consider the mission and the destiny which Providence
seems to have designed for us, and let us so take care of our
own conduct, that, with irreproachable hearts and with
hands void of offense, we may stand up whenever and wherever called upon, and, with a voice not to be disregarded,
say, this shall not be done, at least not without our protest."

XI

A PART OF TRANSYLVANIA COMES BACK*

INTRODUCTION

WHEN ROUMANIA ceded northern Transylvania to Hungary in 1940, the Hungarian Quarterly—published in English in Budapest and reaching a considerable constituency in Hungary, Great Britain, and the United States—devoted an issue to Transylvania, from which this article is taken. It was hoped that the new division of territory would lead to better understanding. The chapter expresses this hope: it is of 1940.

The writer is the author of this book, Louis C. Cornish. For long he was president of the American Unitarian Association, which includes the Unitarian Churches in both the United States and Canada; since 1937 he has been president of the International Association for Liberal Christianity and Religious Freedom, an organization with member groups in twenty-three countries.

He has made journeys of investigation in Transylvania, for more than thirty years he has been well informed concerning its conditions and particularly its churches, and he has tried to help all of them—the Roman Catholic, Prot-

* Hungarian Quarterly, Winter Issue 1940, Vol. VI, No. 4.

estant, and the Jewish Synagogues—to maintain themselves under Roumanian rule, according to the provisions of the treaties and Roumanian statutes established for the protection of the minorities.

I rejoice that a part of Transylvania, torn from Hungary by the Trianon Treaty, is again under Hungarian rule. I love Transylvania, and I know the intolerable oppression her people have suffered under Roumanian rule. I rejoice because it has ended in part of the land. Whatever the sovereignty over it may be in the future, I pray that like suffering never again may come to any of the peoples living in Transylvania.

I refrain from commenting upon past political divisions, or upon the present Roumanian boundary (1940). Neither do I offer any speculations as to what the future may hold. Instead I seize this chance to make an appeal.

Since 1919 I have been deeply concerned about the repression of the Minority Churches in Transylvania. Roman Catholic and Protestant, these institutions both expressed and perpetuated a high civilization. To lay the axe at their roots was a sure method of crippling Hungarian culture. Accordingly it was applied, and has continued to be applied.

Our group of American Unitarian Churches, together with the Unitarian group in Great Britain, from the year 1825, when both groups were formed, down to the beginning of the First World War maintained helpful relations with the Unitarian Churches of Hungary, most of them in Transylvania. Then the relationship was abruptly interrupted. For some time no word passed between us. The frontiers of Transylvania had been sealed. The Roumanian Army, we learned later, had been turned loose in Transylvania. Then rumors of the suffering of the people began to seep through the barriers, and a representative of our churches in the British Empire and the United States penetrated to the very storm center. He got in without the permission of the Roumanian authorities—had he asked it would never have been granted—and he got out on a train that was vainly searched for him. He was hidden in the tender of a locomotive and covered with coal.

Arrived in England safely, he proclaimed what was happening. Roumania did not, perhaps she could not, restrain the newcomers who were being poured into the acquired land. He told the Scotch Presbyterians and the Hierarchy of the American Roman Catholic Church, he told all the churches outside Roumania that were affiliated with the Transylvania Churches. Great interest was aroused, and ever since it has been a smouldering fire, now dull, now flaring.

After these many years it is easy to see that nothing less than a period of ruthlessness, of arbitrary imprisonments, denial of rights of assembly, robbery, and endless petty irritations making life well nigh unendurable, was to have been expected. All this might have been foreseen by the men who sat around the council table and drafted the Trianon Treaty. It was perhaps the worst feature of the Peace Treaties. American influence, through ignorance but nonetheless truly, played its part at the Trianon. Given the human ingredients in Transylvania and Roumania at the time, this long period of unsettlement now appears to have been the inevitable sequence to giving the territory to Bucharest rule.

To make this plain, let us look dispassionately at Roumania, glad of her progress in recent decades in schools, and the rest, but remembering her history. Only in 1878 did her allegiance to Turkey finally end. To Turkey and the East she largely owes her traditions and customs, legal and other. In Hungary, for example, an accused man is considered innocent until proven guilty, in Roumania he is held guilty until he can prove himself innocent. In the first country judges are paid by the state, in the other no judge hears a case until the defendant pays him. This is his source of income. I called this procedure to the attention of a provincial Roumanian Governor. Said he, "Tell me who will pay the judges if the defendants do not!"

It is always to be remembered that Roumania's government at the top has not been essentially Roumanian. Bismarck put the present German royalty on the throne. Of her rulers a heavy preponderance were of Greek descent, often high financiers, whose families came originally from Constantinople. A very few men owned, and still own, great areas leaving the landless masses but little above serfdom. It is glaringly clear that the Roumanian people never have had a chance. Byzantine and Oriental are words often applied to Roumania. She lies to the east and south of the great dividing wall of the Carpathians, while to the north and west of them live the Magyars, Saxons and other races, people of high culture, law-abiding, able. A difference of at least three hundred years in progress separates the two cultures of Roumania and Hungary.

These statements are necessary briefly to explain the fact, and it is not the fault but the misfortune of Roumania, that when she took over Transylvania she lacked the solid, intelligent, informed middle class which she so needed. The Roumanians who poured into the territory had the tradition of their own Turkish experiences. What, pray, is a minority for if it is not to be fleeced? The great and most difficult task of combining the two cultures, if possible even ultimately of amalgamating them, confronted the Roumanians, and their men had neither the education nor the experience which the very difficult occasion demanded.

It might have been expected that following the Roumanian occupation of Transylvania there would be a period of lawlessness, incompetence and tyranny. The farm creatures, horses and cattle, pigs and geese, were freely taken by the invaders, or if you will, by the new masters; chaos reigned and all sorts of personal abuses took place. These happened in a thousand forms. To summarize, I quote from one of my own reports ("Transylvania in 1922"): "The personal abuse of Transylvanian people by Roumanian soldiers and civilians is established beyond the slightest possibility of disproval and must be forever a source of shame to every enlightened Roumanian." So I wrote in 1922, and the passing years have strengthened my conviction of the truth of my statement.

Two questions were much discussed outside Roumania in these early postwar days. Had these abuses of all kinds really happened? Did they continue? Roumanian apologists protested: first, that none of these things ever had happened; and second, all of them had ceased. Somebody must go and learn what was the true situation. So it came about that I was appointed chairman of an Anglo-American commission by the American Committee on the Rights of Minorities to visit Transylvania, investigate and report.

Determined to approach our study with open minds, the commission journeyed by way of Northern Italy and across Yugoslavia to Bucharest. We did not go first to Hungary.

We were courteously received by the Roumanian government officials and encouraged to proceed without supervision or interference. And so we went to Transylvania.

How the pictures of that beautiful land stay with one
through the years! In the valleys were the broad cultivated
fields, behind them rose mountains. The villages were of
whitewashed houses with dull red tiled roofs. Always the
church and school stood dominantly among them. Always
there were men and women in their distinctive dress. Always the bells rang on our coming and oak branches in the
belfries gave welcome, always there was abounding hospitality. Was it possible that hardship and sorrow rode the
land?

We travelled widely, visiting the deaneries and taking
testimony from people of many affiliations. We met them in
out-of-the-way places, sometimes orchards. As they sought
us out men would enter singly from an adjacent field, or
walk warily along the hedges. They were afraid to be seen
with us or to tell us their sufferings, and with reason. Not
long before a foreign publicist, accompanied by a Roumanian official, had taken similar testimony, and the official
had urged the people to speak freely. After the visitor had
departed all who had testified were put in jail, and in various
other ways disciplined. So the witnesses were shy about
talking with us as their minds and hearts prompted. Nonetheless we collected overwhelming and voluminous evidence
of abuses, compiled it, and later published it in part. In no
instance, please mark this, did we talk politics. Ours was
another quest: we wanted certain facts. The only question
that concerned us was whether the stipulations of the Trianon Treaty safeguarding the rights of the Minorities were

being fulfilled by the Roumanian Government. We were driven to the conclusion that they were not being fulfilled; instead they were being flouted.

What we saw and felt with these people never can be adequately transferred to other minds by statistical reports. Let your imagination interpret a few of the cases.

A weeping woman and her husband stood with me before their little field, its crop ripe for harvesting. The Roumanian chief official of the village had told them that morning that thereafter the field was to be his, and without payment. Never would it again be theirs. It was their only field. To his mind there was nothing legal or illegal in this procedure. He wanted the land and took it. It was as simple as that! It meant ruin to the farmer.

A young widow asked my help. Her husband had been killed in an American coal mine. She was entitled to a small pension from the mine owners which she bitterly needed. It would have had far greater purchasing power there than in America. The death had been attested, the documents had been sent her, all that was lacking was the signature of the local magistrate with hers. He had refused to sign unless she promised to give him one-half of her pension payment permanently. No doubt this official had paid the official above him for his appointment, now he was collecting his living off the people under him. It was the Roumanian way. The woman had refused, she would receive nothing unless and until she consented, and despite her protests the official had kept the papers.

Another needy widow testified. Her husband's body had been brought from a neighboring town for burial. Down the line the flat car carrying the coffin had been switched to a siding. Remember that it is hot in Transylvania in the summer. The woman succeeded in getting the car attached to another train only after she had paid the local official a substantial sum, no doubt scraped together by her friends.

If people wished to leave Cluj-Kolozsvar they must get permission from the local authorities, which was not required by the law. Women went day after day, Roumanian as well as Magyar women, carrying their gifts, sometimes poultry, sometimes bedding, for they had no money. Some of them were kept waiting for a month, while they made their daily visits, and brought their pitiful bribes, in order to obtain permission to do what they had the right to do without either permission or payment.

There were such incidents without number. We had little testimony of personal beatings, and the like. Due in part perhaps to an aroused world public opinion these had largely ceased. Everywhere, however, peculation was the order of the day, elevated if you will into a sort of regulation affair for the support of the ascending tiers of Roumanian officials.*

It may be well to inquire if these abuses were known to the top people in Bucharest. They were! Here is an example. The ranking official of a great denomination, widely scattered throughout Christendom, told me that in an interview with Queen Marie about 1920 he had said to her in effect, Your Majesty has a tremendous opportunity to make a name for yourself in world history by showing yourself a friend to the oppressed minorities. Her Majesty replied in effect that she had to be concerned first with what the Roumanians thought of her.

Here is another example. The wife of a titled Hungarian—his name is known internationally—told me that

* See account of Roumanian "Phanariote Financial System," Chap. XIV.

she sent to Queen Marie by the hand of one of her Majesty's ladies-in-waiting a description of a case of crying cruelty, and implored her royal influence for mercy. A few days later a note was delivered at this lady's door. On a plain sheet of note paper, without address, or date or signature, was written in what appeared to be the Queen's hand, "My heart breaks, but my hands are tied."*

There were constant protests against minority abuses from within Transylvania, and from many parts of the world besides, some far distant. There were formal protests to the League of Nations and considerations, always informal, by League members. When Queen Marie made her visit to the United States, a monster petition on behalf of the Transylvanian Minorities, praying for their protection under the guarantees of the Trianon Treaty, was in process of circulation throughout the United States, and was rolling up thousands of signatures when the Queen went home. The petition was in due course delivered at the Roumanian Le-

* *Hungarian Quarterly,* Chap. XI, p. 9.

The peace loving world was indifferent to these happenings, so it appeared. They were common enough in Transylvania and other transferred territories. Those concerned cried out, few heard. The League of Nations did nothing, nobody did anything. And here is the point of it all, such abuses grew in intensity and number because they went unrebuked. The world knew that the protection of minorities agreed on in the treaties was totally disregarded. The international brigands believed that nobody ever would really stand up to them. Hitler planned only on a short war. Had world righteousness been implemented to strike in rebuke when these outrages were few and new, they gradually would have ceased. The poor widow without her pension, another waiting for the funeral of her husband, the man and wife standing before the field of which they had been robbed take on more importance when we remember that they represented millions of other sufferers who might have been spared their martyrdoms if only the United Nations organization had existed and functioned. There was no one adequately to rebuke such abuses, which were allowed to become widespread.

gation in Washington. There has been no lack of witnesses to Roumanian oppression of minorities.

In 1924 I again visited Transylvania as chairman of another Anglo-American Commission sent by the same American Committee to investigate and report on the treatment of the minorities. The Commission again journeyed directly to Bucharest. We were graciously entertained by the King and Queen, were courteously received by the high officials of the Government, and were told that if we would submit a written report of our findings the Government would reply.

After prolonged investigation the Commission submitted a memorandum to the High Ministers of State of the Roumanian Government.* It begins:

"Several Commissions concerned with the welfare of the four churches formerly supported by the Hungarian State have visited Transylvania since 1919, representing the affectionate interest felt by the sister churches of the Transylvanian Lutheran, Presbyterian or Reformed, Roman Catholic, and Unitarian Churches, throughout the British Empire and the United States. These Commissions have failed to be satisfied that the Roumanian Government has yet fulfilled the provisions of the Trianon Treaty guaranteeing the rights of the Minority Churches. Their reports have been widely circulated in both the British Empire and the United States, and have caused much comment unfavourable to Roumania."

The Commission then presented minority difficulties under five groups: I. The new law compelling societies to submit their statutes to the Ministry, and to obtain permission to hold meetings; II. Alleged cases of personal abuse on the

* "Religious Minorities in Transylvania," Louis C. Cornish.

part of Roumanian officials; III. The rights of the confessional schools; IV. The loss of lands owned by the churches; and V. Other alleged cases of interference with the rights of minorities guaranteed by Roumania in her acceptance of the terms of the Trianon Treaty.

We submitted 135 alleged cases of abuse, selected from an enormous mass of evidence, not as peculiar but as symptomatic. The Roumanian Government denied all but two cases, these are not the most important. In one instance only, and at this point the text of the reply is not clear, was redress given. Questions regarding policy were evaded. In certain of its denials, however, the Roumanian Government made large and significant admissions. In Case D (p. 111, "Religious Minorities in Transylvania"), the government admitted that any person whose name a local official might arbitrarily decide to be Roumanian origin could be coerced against his will and judgment to unite with the Greek Orthodox or Roumanian Church. Large Greek Orthodox churches have been built where there were few Roumanians to use them, and large numbers of non-Roumanian people have been driven into them, despite the fact that complete religious freedom is one of the stipulations of the Trianon Treaty. It was deliberately flouted, or quite forgotten. I quote the conclusion of our report:

"The (Roumanian) High Ministers of State in conference with the Commission acknowledged certain abuses; for example, where the Unitarian College was penalized by one department (of the Roumanian Government) for obeying another department; and again where the Presbyterian Kunn College met with severe losses and was closed. The High Ministers of State promised relief. The reply shows that nothing has been done.

"One constant complaint which the Minorities made to the Commission was that abuses are presented to the Bucharest Government with all details, are listened to sympathetically, and relief is promised. Then nothing whatever is done. This is the treatment accorded the Commission's memorandum, written at the request of the Roumanian Government. . . . The reply of the Government is evasive and inconclusive."

Through all these following years I have watched the continuing struggle for the rights of freedom against greed and tyranny center around a few large matters. The Minority schools have been weakened and in many places closed, and the children driven into public schools of inferior quality often controlled by the local Greek Orthodox priest, and used by him for ecclesiastical instruction. In applying agrarian reform, the reapportionment of the vast estates into small peasant holdings, the endowment lands slowly acquired for the schools and churches have been largely confiscated, despite the fact that they did not fall into the recognized categories. All minority institutions, pinched here, retarded there, always harassed and perplexed, and often penalized by conflicting orders received from the distant offices in Bucharest, through these years have been submitted to a process of attrition, deliberately applied with the intention of eventually killing them.

When King Ferdinand was entertaining our Commission, he said to me, "You are interested in these minorities; remember that within a generation they will be Roumanians, or else" and he significantly touched the hilt of his sword.

"May I express an opinion?" I asked. Royal assent having been given, I said, "I have been to Sibiu, and the Saxons there are as Saxon today as they were seven hundred years ago." His Majesty literally gave me the cold shoulder. He walked away without replying. His word and gesture accidentally showed the real attitude of the Roumanian Government. By this way and that, by ever-changing methods, by the attrition of institutions, by taking away the land from the minorities, now under one pretext, now under another, by driving the people into the State Church there to be directed by the Greek Orthodox priest, by substituting strange tales for history in the schools, and by promoting the emigration of all Hungarians who could be made to leave the country, by every conceivable method the effort has been made to make Transylvania Roumanian, so thoroughly racially that it would stay Roumanian politically.

What books might be written on the subject of these forced migrations! Robbed of their land, evicted, what could people do except migrate! Arrived at the border, they were refused passports, and were not allowed to cross until they were starved into going without them. Contemplate trying in these days to migrate without money, without citizenship in the land you are leaving behind, and then seeking to enter any other country. Mexico, to her great credit, took pity on one such group, partly composed of Magyar professional people. At long last they found themselves in Mexico City, where several of them died, utterly spent. The Mexican climate and labor conditions made it hard for them to remain. Being without passports and without a possible quota assignment, we in the United States could do nothing for them. I had a hand in getting them finally to Canada, and there the survivors have found refuge, and have made new homes. The ghastly pity of it all! Disrupt a civilization, in a land like Transylvania, and the people pay and pay and pay with anguish and blood and death. Put out a huge ruthless hand on a people, press down a little harder now here and now there, and keep pressing down and down, and all around the edges of the land you spill out tragedy, inevitably.

At the Trianon council table the pendulum swung far out of beat for Hungary. Now (1940) it has swung back part way. What does the swing-back mean for all peoples? "We Roumanians," said one of them to me in Transylvania, "have been the lower classes, looked down on by the Magyars, held of little account, denied our common rights, and it is our turn." Whether or not his accusations are true is incidental to our purpose; the words give a viewpoint. His meaning is plain. Now the Roumanians are on top, and they intend to stay there. So far as they are able they will grind in the dust the faces of all the other peoples. As the King said to me, "They will become Roumanians."

The pendulum has swung part way back, and in a part of Transylvania the Roumanians will no longer be on top. But is it not possible that some new equilibrium can be attained so that all the races may be, not amalgamated, but harmonized? Roughly speaking, more than one-half the Transylvanians are Roumanians. The statistics are in endless dispute. Exact figures are not important; it is enough to recognize that the two major races, Magyar and Roumanian, are approximately equal in Transylvania, the Roumanians in the lead, and it is evident that they have got to live together. This last fact is dominant. Here the races are, inextricably shuffled, mixed together.

Must the pendulum forever swing back and forth, now one people in the ascendancy and then the other? Grant that there is ample cause for the Magyars and Saxons and all the other peoples in Transylvania to hate the Roumanians, it remains that all the Roumanians are not bad folk, far from it. It was largely only the Roumanian officialdom that has given the Transylvanians cause for hatred. What is to follow? Will the minority peoples, robbed, abused, and misgoverned as they have been for twenty years, now take their turn treating the Roumanians as the Roumanians treated them? Is the pendulum always to swing back and forth, one race in the saddle and then thrown in the dust? We do not believe it is anybody's intention to do this, but given the human ingredients there is danger. Stability, justice, and peace is the recognized ideal.

Let us look to the possibilities involved. Had the Roumanian Government dealt fairly for these past two decades with the peoples in their newly acquired territory there would now be a very different attitude toward it. Lord Bryce told us long ago that a nation's treatment of its minorities is the acid test of its civilization. If the new government (1940) of the Hungarian part of Transylvania will show restraint, tempering justice with mercy, remembering the common concern in good government instead of the past differences between the races, then the old time Roumanian citizens of Transylvania will be comforted, and the new Roumanian Transylvanian citizens will be happier under the new Transylvanian rule than they ever were under the late Roumanian. Further, and in the day we are enduring it is an act of faith even to think it, upon the sympathetic treatment of all its minorities may ultimately depend the permanence of the new Hungarian Transylvania regime. It is then no less than imperative that the new government set up so adequate a modus vivendi that all races will desire to stay within its recently returned part of Transylvania, and that those outside will wish to come in.

In these past years I have done what I could to help the Transylvanian Minority Churches of every name to secure and maintain their rights under the Trianon Treaty. My heart has been particularly in that land. Perhaps this gives me the privilege of offering advice to the Magyars who will read this plea. If it does, then I hurl my advice with all my might. Make friends with the Roumanians within your borders, those who dwell beside you. Treat them not only with justice, but with mercy. You and they are bound together inextricably, as you have been for long. You now have the chance to set a high standard of human rights. Remember it was in Transylvania, at the Diet of Torda in 1568, for the first time in history it was written into law that no man should be persecuted for his religious opinion. This is one chief glory of your history. I know that you will intend to observe all this, but nonetheless it will be hard, demanding all your courage and patience. But the personal matters, the schools, the colleges, the churches, their lands, their procedures, indeed and indeed how many readjustments are before you! In the times ahead you will be moved by Magyar impulse and tradition. It will be well for all of us who love Transylvania to remember that the honored Crown of St. Stephen carries the symbol of sacrifice and brotherhood: it is surmounted by the Cross.

XII

AN IMPERATIVE PROBLEM

by

ARPAD ARVAY

INTRODUCTION

THREE YEARS after the last chapter was published in the Hungarian Quarterly, 1940, the following speech was made in the Hungarian Parliament, on November 26, 1943, by the Hon. Arpad Arvay. It tells what has been happening in the interval, and shows that the hopes expressed in the earlier statement had not been realized.

The solution of the Hungarian-Roumanian question is the most difficult problem whose early solution is imperative for the Hungarian Government. Many reports and data inform us how the Hungarians, there are hundreds of thousands of them living under Roumanian domination, are obliged to endure completely intolerable conditions, although we had long since concluded many peaceful agreements and had made all possible efforts.

It is a curious fact that the Roumanian State, which had to pay with the collapse of its constitution and with considerable territorial loss for its ill treatment of the minorities,

even today continues to choose oppression rather than understanding. The great powers which acted as umpires between Hungary and Roumania obliged both countries to
give the minorities under their rule legal rights and possibilities to live. In Hungary these obligations of the Vienna
award, as we know, have been scrupulously fulfilled many
times and even far beyond the actual obligations. It is to be
regretted that this patient attitude has not found any echo
from the other side. Roumania has continued its policy of
oppression, not only toward the Hungarians but toward all
other minorities under her rule. It should not be forgotten
that since the Vienna award Roumania has not only accepted particular obligations toward the Hungarians, but
also toward her German minorities. It is only with these
facts before us that we can understand the full measure of
the injustice meted out to the hundreds of thousands of
Hungarians who are forced to live under Roumanian domination. Day after day we receive reports that are more and
more shocking. These show that the situation of the Hungarians under Roumanian domination has now become absolutely impossible. Those who know Roumanian "justice"
understand that the "laws" are made in Roumania in such
a disorderly manner that they can always be used against
a minority. There are financial laws, for instance, so constructed as to become traps, and the Hungarian peasants,
industrialists, tradesmen, and workers fall into them, even
against their best intentions. These laws are worded so that
the determination on an infringement, as well as the final
judgment, are made by the same executive officials, who act
under secret instructions. No proof to the contrary of the
charge is admitted as evidence. Thus it comes about that
Hungarians are punished in a way that means their com-

plete material ruin. We are informed that Hungarian firms, or Hungarian tradesmen, who had been operating for decades have had to close down their business because of these financial regulations. There is also the so-called "Sabotage-Law" which just recently has been strengthened exceedingly against the Southern Transylvanian Hungarians. Under this law there is no legal evidence against the protocol decision of the executive officials. These officials, sent especially for the purpose, can at will establish such protocol decisions, not only against Hungarian industrialists and tradesmen, but also even against the market peddlers. These protocols charge the victims with such grave crimes that they result in the confiscation of all their property, and also generally bring a punishment, perhaps several years in a penitentiary. The unfortunate Hungarians are either ruined or sent to jail, or in their desperation they somehow manage to escape across the border.

The Roumanian authorities have lately concentrated on the farmers. With unbelievable cruelty they have been confiscating the cattle. They carry away even the last animal, and the farmers receive nothing in compensation, or such a small sum that it is insufficient even to pay the transfer tax. The Roumanian authorities confiscating the animals pay in the best cases only 3 filler (0.07 cent per 2 pounds) per kilogram.

This situation has now gone so far that a member of the Hungarian minority in Roumania can no longer be a Government official, a tradesman, an industrialist, or even a worker. If by a miracle a member of the minority still finds employment somewhere, then there comes the so-called labor-camp with all its horrors. In these labor-camps thousands of Hungarians are living in unbelievable misery, dirt and starvation. They are not only men in their best age, but also young men between 17 and 18 and old men between 67 and 69 years of age.

Another example: the Roumanians for several years have been building the railroad line Deva-Bradi. In this dreary country 1,600 Hungarians have been called in for labor, mostly people around 50 years of age. These men must work together with the convicts condemned to from ten to fifteen years of hard labor, and the treatment accorded them and the convicts is the same.

Even worse is the situation of those Hungarians conscripted for labor in the Szurdok valley. Six thousand Hungarians work there, and look forward to the winter with terror. Last winter there was in the labor-camp a group of Russian prisoners of war. Their dwellings were only barracks made of light wooden planks. Consequently almost all of the Russian prisoners of war froze to death. The cemetery of these unfortunate victims is at the doors of the barracks where the Hungarians now live. They are infested with vermin, suffer from many communicable diseases and are kept on the verge of starvation. The Roumanian guards cynically call the camp "Cimitirul ungrilor," which means "Cemetery of the Hungarians."

And these labor services do not last only for two or three weeks. Very often they go on for ten or twelve months, and during that time the family at home receives no compensation or support whatever. In most cases, the family's business has been destroyed and goes into bankruptcy. It often happens that when the Hungarians finally return, they do not find the women members of their families, because since

October 1943 even the women have been called into labor-camps. Young girls and even mothers with young children have been called in besides older women. For example, all dressmakers and needleworkers, mostly young girls from Torda, have been ordered to Nagyszeben to work for the soldiers. I need not stress what has happened to these unfortunate girls in the barracks of the unrestrained Roumanian soldiers.

To top all this the Roumanian authorities have ordered that so-called refugee Roumanian families can be established in every house belonging to members of the minority. It has happened frequently that Hungarians have been suddenly moved from their houses in order to make place for the so-called refugees. All of which shows that the Hungarians are not equal-righted citizens in Roumania. Indeed, they enjoy no rights at all.

On the basis of official information we could continue endlessly to enumerate instances of the abuse of the Hungarian minority under Roumanian domination. But these few facts which I bring to your attention are sufficient to show how this situation can no longer continue.

When exposing the situation I want to appeal to Roumanian public opinion. Roumanians cannot forget, whether they want them or not, they have common interests with the other Danubian nations. In this decisive hour they should understand that it is for their own interest to change their attitude toward their neighbors. The Hungarians do not want to exploit the tragic, nay the desperate situation, in which Roumania finds herself. If the Roumanians are ready to treat the Hungarians decently there is still a chance to find ground for collaboration.

This speech delivered in '43 is typical of abundant testimony to the same effect, and gives a vivid picture of recent minority sufferings, and of the relations between the two countries. It is published here for the first time in English.

XIII

WOE

THE stormy wind
Rushes through the dusky night
And through the forest
Roaring and rumbling.

On the peaks of the haughty cliffs
Hell is foaming.
Abruptly, the strife ceases
Ceases suddenly,
And from the wounded, bleeding
Valley and cliffs
Clang the sonorous, warm,
Virgin-pure sounds
Where in this great primeval forest
Hides in secret the interred
Hungarian bell.

Golden bell, dear bell
Embracing words mingle
With the exhausted worn-out night,
Thy tones shine, and kindle a night lamp,
And shake us inwardly.

Or is it the voice of millions of hearts
That sounds with dignity?

Thou mutilated earth,
Torn and clawed into four parts,
Oh! Bleed not to death, bleed not to death!
It is not the last, it is not an endless night.
By Christ's five wounds
I say this,
I say this!

On the enslaved mountains
In the wild storm
Deep and wonderful,
Belief is once again born.

(A part of "The Hungarian Bell" by Stephen Havas, taken from "Hungarian Heroes of Liberty," p. 23, printed in Budapest, without copyright.)

XIV

WHAT DIFFERENCE DOES IT MAKE?

WHAT DIFFERENCE does it make whether Hungary or Roumania rules Transylvania? Or she becomes autonomous in some larger federation?

What difference would it make to Californians if they were ceded to Mexico? Life in the United States derives from free-choice emigration, education well considered and compulsory, the common law, representative government, and religious freedom. Our people are largely descended from the northern European races. And Mexico is another story. By ruthless conquest the Mexican native civilization was taken over by Spain, her people still are preponderantly Indian, illiteracy is general, Spanish law is the foundation of Mexican legal development. Mexican parliamentary procedure, to speak gently, has been more colorful than the American. One great Church dominates, and controls an amazing amount of the best land and other forms of wealth. Mexico differs from twentieth century California in tradition, language, law, and custom. It would make a very great difference to Californians if Mexico ruled them. This is said with all respect for Mexico. The development of the two countries stems from different cultures.

But California never could be given to Mexico! Probably not, since she belongs to a blessed union of free states. However, the suggestion may help us understand that something vital happened to the Magyars and Saxons in Transylvania and also to the Roumanians long resident there, when following the First World War, as a bribe to Roumania to bring her into the war on the side of the Allies, and nobody asking their opinion, they were passed over to Bucharest rule, the Hungarian protests and arguments against the procedure not even considered at Versailles where the decision to give Transylvania to Roumania already had been made before the delegates from Hungary arrived, all this with the United States consenting and participating. It is an ugly picture. Shall we create another like it? That part of Transylvania which Roumania gave back to Hungary in 1940, is now turned over again to Roumania, and the Saxon and Magyar Transylvanians must live under Roumanian rule permanently, or until another upheaval shall free them, and once more set Europe on fire.

Is there no other alternative for Transylvania except Hungarian or Roumanian rule? In the name of suffering humanity, is there no other way forward and out, not forgetting to help Roumania? The freedom-loving United Nations must realize how it makes a life-and-death difference to the Magyars and Saxons of Transylvania to be given permanently to Roumania, and it also makes the same difference to the long established Roumanians who have no love for Bucharest rule. The Russian-Roumanian armistice provides for reconsideration of its decisions, which needs to be kept in the foreground. Roumanian propaganda tells how in former days they were oppressed by the Magyars.

Whether true or not, this is aside from the point. If a third alternative were offered, might not they prefer it?

What are the main differences between Roumania and Hungary? They are geographical and historical. Mountain ranges have protected the thousand year long development of Hungarian life. No sheltering mountains surround old Roumania. Upon three sides she is without natural barriers, and particularly to the east her lands lie wide open. Endlessly aliens have trampled on her. The Greeks at Constantinople long ruled and robbed her,* then came the Turks with equally oppressive policies. She continued to be a province of Turkey until the Treaty of Berlin made her independent in 1878. Bulgaria fell to the Turks in 1371, Wallacia—now part of Roumania—appears on Turkey's list of vassal states in 1391.† To sum up the history of the centuries that intervene between those days and our own times, it suffices to point out that the setup of the present political Roumania is but of yesterday compared with the more than thousand-year experience and discipline of much of Hungary: geography and history cannot be ignored.

It has been assumed far too easily that there was little difference for the Magyars, Saxons, and Transylvanian Roumanians between living under Roumanian or Hungarian rule. Or does nobody care? Such experiences and comparisons arising from them lie far outside the living problems of Americans. They think little of moving about between the states. But what happened when a Magyar village passed under Roumanian rule? Or a Saxon village?

* "It was at this period," writes Aricescu, Roumanian historian, "that the Roumanian peasant became a sheep, fleeced, milked, and finally skinned by the Greek interloper."
† See Seton Watson, History of Roumania, p. 33.

Children were forced to leave the Hungarian schools with their excellent government supervised curriculum under thoroughly well trained teachers and their nine months sessions, and enter Roumanian schools continuing for a much shorter period, in some places for a few weeks only, where Roumanian was the chief language used if not the only one, where the curriculum consisted largely of the lives of the saints and the catechism of the Roumanian Church, and all of this under the direct supervision and often under the personal teaching of the local, poorly educated priest. The Roumanian substitute in education was nothing like as good as the Hungarian which it superseded. A Scotch educator, who spoke Magyar and was familiar with the schools throughout Hungary, considered the Magyar-Saxon schools abreast of the best schools in Britain and the United States.

This difference in educational standards and methods derives from the differences in the historical development of Hungary and Roumania.

Hungary endured the Turks for a century and a half; and lost vast numbers of her people; so did Roumania only she was forced to endure them for five centuries. The invasions rent Hungary into three parts, the western came under the Emperors, the Turks held the center, and on the east Transylvania became an independent principality for a century and a half, becoming the center of Magyar and Saxon culture. But Roumania had no respite. She had no mountain state that held out.

Here is an example of the Turkish point of view toward her victims in both countries. In giving an order for rye, "The Lord and Master of the Mighty Turkish Emperor's border fortress of Eger" addresses certain Magyars: "You headsmen, disobedient dogs, hounds and pigs, bring us two cartloads of rye. For if you fail to do so I shall descend on you with a few thousand of my men and empale some of you and so treat the rest that even the milk that they sucked at their mother's breast shall turn sour in their stomachs." The bombast about a few thousand men, and this no doubt conventional form of order to the unarmed people of the countryside, show us intended and practiced brutality. No doubt the master of Eger got his rye.

When the Turks ruled Hungary thousands of Magyars were driven into exile, thousands more were killed or died of want. Not forgetting the fearful Turkish devastations in Hungary, it was one but only one horrible chapter. For Roumania Turkish invasion was one long continuous suffering, from 1391 to 1878. Before pointing to certain facts relevant to our consideration we pause to pay tribute to Roumania's advance on certain lines during these past decades. Since the First World War she has spent lavishly on training teachers, and she has been generous to her universities. And she has trudged along the hard road of advance with many difficulties. Yet the differences of cultural level, bluntly named of civilization, must be faced.

The law of the two countries is profoundly different, the one is Oriental, the other Occidental. Financial methods differ, that of Roumania being a Turkish inheritance. In the old days, let us say, it became known that the Sultan was about to send a new governor to Roumania. Men bid for the appointment, and offered all they could, and when the fortunate appointee arrived at his government he recouped himself. Every official down the ladder to the last petty officer collected off the people. Many of the appointees were Greeks from the Phanariote district of Constantinople, and the whole system is often called by their name.

The system remains in effect. "Squeeze" is not the bare cupidity of individuals. It is a system, familiar in the East, and not unknown in the West although practiced under cover. Deplore it as we may, it is a system. We meet it in Roumania, and in Roumanian Transylvania.

Take political life in the Transylvanian villages. Public office among Magyars and Saxons meant honor and responsibility, with little compensation, or none; but under Roumanian rule it has meant "squeeze." In his native land, before he came into Transylvania, the petty Roumanian officer knew nothing else. He paid somebody higher up for his appointment, now he must collect. Don't think too harshly of the ticket seller as an individual, annoying as overpayment for an extra visa on your passport may be. You are under a system of the East, when you have been accustomed to another system of the West. Until recent years no inkling of responsibility on the part of governors for the welfare of the governed ever entered a Turkish head. It is not common now. What a fatuous notion! What is new territory for, indeed, if it is not to be squeezed? What is a minority for if it is not to be fleeced? At bottom squeeze is a barter system, eastern and ancient.

No greater difference exists between Roumania and Hungary than in their churches. In Transylvania, at the Diet of Torda in 1568 you will remember that for the first time in history religious liberty was written into law: it was forced on Roumania in 1878 by the Treaty of Berlin. The Roumanian Constitution recognizes religious liberty, but only

in theory, not in practice but on paper. In fact the Roumanian Greek Orthodox Church is dominant and becomes
an instrument of oppression. It differs profoundly from the
Roman Catholic and Protestant Churches of the West. It is
fixed in its formalism and unchangeable theology, both of
which are obviously its own affair. But when it enters politics then its activities become the affair of the entire people,
and even of the surrounding states.

In Transylvania this Roumanian Greek Orthodox Church
has been in endless ways intrusive. In a Transylvanian
town, for example, a visiting commission investigating the
Roumanian treatment of minorities found the Roumanian
Greek Orthodox Church occupying a building adjacent to
a Magyar sixteenth century Protestant Church. A wooden
scaffolding had been put up under one of the chancel windows. On it a good sized bell had been hung which was rung
regularly during the Sunday morning meetings in the
church. There was no call for it to be rung at this hour, no
masses were being said; it was sounded merely to be a nui-
sance to a Magyar congregation.

As a means to transform the minority peoples into Roumanians the Roumanian authorities in Transylvanian villages have forced large numbers of people against their will
into the Roumanian Greek Orthodox Church. But why?
Roumania promises freedom of religion to all her citizens.
What has the derivation of your surname to do with it?
Everything imaginable! If the authorities claim that once
your surname was Roumanian, whether their conclusion be
true or not, into the Roumanian Church you go, or you
suffer penalties of all sorts, including the ruin of your business and the suffering of your family. In free countries you

could choose for yourself: not in Roumania. Religious freedom there is wholly theory, not practice.*

Roumanian rule in Transylvania has meant slow, persistent, planned attrition of minority life. How many examples could be cited! There were the deaneries, ministers' associations we should call them in the United States, small regional ministerial groups having some administrative responsibility and representation in the denominational councils. Roumanian authorities in certain Transylvanian localities arbitrarily regrouped the churches, making the deaneries extend on both sides of the mountains. On paper this seemed harmless enough. But journeys over or around the mountains were too long and too costly to be practicable. As had been planned no meetings of the deaneries could be held. There has been constant interference with all the minority churches, Protestant and Roman Catholic, and with the Jewish synagogues, also with the schools and colleges, with the rights of assembly and free speech, and throughout there has been endless peculation. There is no lack of testimony about the pressure on the minorities by the Roumanian overlords.

Hitler forced Roumania to return the northern forty percent of Transylvania to Hungary, and not by accident set the new boundary line in the middle of the plain where it could not be easily defended. He had to make an adjustment of Transylvanian territory or have an Hungarian-Roumanian war on his hands just when Germany was depending on the Roumanian oil-fields for at least one third of her fighting oil supply: he was no Santa Claus making a gift to his prisoner, Hungary.

* See "The Religious Minorities in Transylvania," by Louis C. Cornish, p. III.

It was hoped by all the friends of Transylvania that this transfer of her territory and sovereignty would not hurt the peoples on either side of the new border. More explicitly, it was hoped that Roumanians with Hungarian jurisdiction newly established over them in the northern forty per cent of Transylvania would remain undisturbed, and that the Magyars and Saxons left in the southern part of Transylvania under Roumanian rule would be treated with consideration. Instead, to the south of the new line there was increased suffering. No less than 20,000 people, largely Magyars, were driven off their farms, beaten up, and forced across the new boundary where hospitals were packed with the seriously injured.

What difference does it make who rules Transylvania? Here are some of the answers to the question, which could be amplified endlessly. Says Havas, "Hell is foaming." And through all the incidents the sequence is plain; one race up and the other down. Such was the effect of Hitler's redivision; now his decision has been upset and is referred to the Peace Conference; one race down and the other up. For the peace of these two beautiful lands, and of the world, for the welfare of these two important races, and of the Transylvanian Saxons with them, all this heaving to and fro must give place to some real equilibrium that can bring hope and good will. It is of course as important that the Roumanians live comfortably and progress in Transylvania as it is for the Magyars and Saxons to enjoy these privileges. These peoples should go forward together. And this is not impossible if only a system of spontaneous cooperation is organized, based on freedom and self determination.

Constant unrest, enmity, tides of irritation, destroy trade, throttle economic development, and both Roumania and

Hungary are rich lands in their resources. The peoples of a Danubian Federation, relieved of all their trade barriers and jealous restrictions and allowed free economic development could all live in collaboration far better than they ever can separated in bickering rivalries.

XV

PROPULSION, A NEW PLANET

WE SHALL fly across the ocean in a few hours. This is fact not fancy and it is gigantically significant; if only we have the adequate mental facilities we must comprehend all it means. Our minds have got to wrestle with new planetary facts, for much that was once important in our thinking has been left far astern, much that was undreamed of looms ahead, and we are approaching the tall cliffs of the future with the speed of light. Old separations between countries, mountains and rivers, seas and continents, dwindle to rivulets and hummocks on the shores of eternity. New unities loom ahead.

One obstacle to understanding what is happening is the poverty of our languages, our words are neither big nor quick enough. The concepts of distance and separation they convey are fruitfully inadequate. Provincialism in all its million forms has been hoisted as by some miracle and without warning to the top of the Tower of Babel, where everybody shouts but nobody comprehends. We are only beginning to realize that humanity is taking on a new sphere of being.

Think back a little, we were born land creatures. For

long, the scientists tell us, we have been standing up on our hind legs and looking about us. Cosmically speaking the habit is recent, quite too late to do anything about it! We wanted to discover things so we walked around. We came to the edge of the sea. We got astride a log and started. We paddled, we sailed, we made ourselves engines, and still eager and questing we have now made ourselves wings.

In the three decades that we have been travelling aloft we have written a whole literature for the world of the sky is new to us. Many questions must be answered. In war we climb into the stratosphere to escape bullets from the ground, but in peace will there be any advantage in our doing so? These high flights cost tremendous sums for equipment, pressurized cabins, oxygen masks, special clothing and the like, and fuel; in times of peace will such high flights be profitable? Now we fly heavily loaded at about 10,000 feet, roughly two miles up; without too much strain we can fly at 25,000 feet, just under five miles, and with effort even higher. Speed constantly increases; what about future speed, a decade or several decades from now? What about directions? An aviator flying over Europe can get phone instructions from London. The coordination of things big and little in aviation, signals, airfields, rules of the road, shows that affairs in the air world are settling into routine, which is constantly readapting itself to new demands. The record of yesterday is nothing to the record of today. And along with this development there is the evidence of increasing world unity and consciousness of world accessibility. We find it in the new histories, in the arts and in the sciences. Even international menace takes on planetary dimensions. Germany did not plan merely to conquer

Europe, she planned to dominate the world, literally and completely.* It was a damnable assumption, but global. Against it is flung the new slogan "One World or None." Mastery of the air involves such changes as we have not yet begun to realize.

Your eyes slip along readily enough over these statements, yet your attention wanders off to other matters; you wonder if you locked the garage. In Heaven's name concentrate on the meaning of our air conquest. Would that we had some mighty planetary form of speech that could force us all to concentrate on it, to rivet our attention upon it. It has tremendous meaning for world federation. Somehow we must become far more deeply aware of the meaning of this new booming of eternity. We men living on this planet are really a single tribe which includes all men everywhere, and this is not sentiment but fact. Science finds only four types of blood and these are universally distributed in all races, together with the O type which is common to all. There is no escaping the fact that the human races are no more than variations of one human stock caused by unnumbered centuries of differing environmental pressures. Men on the polar ice-caps and at the equator are really one; we see the differences due to environment, we ignore the broad unities. All men everywhere make the same noises with our little hammers and whistles. We build the same sort of boats, bows and sterns, sails and engines, to voyage over the seven seas. And now something new has happened, astounding, disruptive, all inclusive, we have taken off into the air, all of us. We, members of the one human tribe, who have been discussing love, and religion, and work and poli-

* On the march German troops sang, "This year Europe, Tomorrow the world."

tics, for these past million years, have recently in a mere tick of the cosmic clock, begun the earth over to talk about flying, and to fly. Above the whole din of affairs a new noise can be heard. Everywhere on the planet men are shouting, "Our world is one world! Our world is one world!"

We are crying, "Where any more are the ends of the earth? Where are our old localisms, and prejudices, our ignorances and hatreds? How meaningless our regional differences and languages are becoming. Where are the mountains that shut us off from our enemies, and the rivers and oceans that divided us? Beneath these questions, as the oceans stretch beneath the cloudbanks, the winds carry the murmur of our new chant, "Our world is one world!"

Yonder, above all the millions of mankind, rises the great high altar of man's faith, lighted with the tall candles of his hope, their flames bending as the winds that blow between the worlds sweep over them, yet never extinguished. Can we rise to planetary consciousness? Shall we ever be eased from the pain and incessant frictions of our diversity? Can it mount into unity? What happens if we fail?

The cathedral we love is nothing more than stones held in high design by mortar, and prayer, and time. How many have crumbled away, how many remain, how many are building and will be building. Curious, but the ideal our cathedral embodies is imperishable. When destroyed, men always build it anew, perhaps not on the same spot, or out of the same rubble; but our cathedral gets itself built again. The ideal it embodied once more takes on substance and form. It lives. Somebody gathered a few stones from the side of the road and began to build: always somebody collects a few stones and builds.

So it is with great achievements. Some man trudging

along the road of experience stumbles on a few facts. Newton watched steam lift the lid of the teakettle. Franklin brought electricity down from his kite. Trying to fly men hurled themselves off towers, like "Darius Green and his flying machine" and wise men laughed. Attempts at flying were ridiculed and forgotten, yet they persisted. Other men trudging along the same roads found the same facts, they too gathered a few stones, and began building.

Almost before we knew it the air age was upon us. Whoever writes the story of aviation works on a tale that will never be finished. No sooner is the great airship B-29 aloft than inventors are working on something to supersede it. No doubt twenty-five years hence everything that now amazes us will be antiquated and put aside. Yet just for comparison's sake we must state a few facts.

In 1903 the Wright brothers got a ramshackle contraption off the ground for one minute. In 1908 their plane stayed in the air for one hour, and aviators in other lands were also beginning to fly.

Skipping many chapters in aviation, in 1944 the ocean-going superfortress B-29 appeared, its wingspread being one hundred and forty feet, the same distance that the Wright brothers' first plane flew. This B-29 can aim from high altitudes with pinpoint accuracy. More men and money have been employed on its improvement than on any other war machine. Seven hundred and fifty engineers worked for two years on its original design. In 1945 one thousand engineers were perfecting it. It carries five thousand numbered parts. It can fly without landing for three thousand miles, perhaps under certain favorable conditions somewhat farther, carrying a load of sixty-five thousand pounds, of which twenty thousand may be bombs. Such fortresses cost one million dollars each. Extraordinary as this B-29 may be, however, it is certain that even more powerful aircraft will surpass it. The jet plane, now in the earlier stages of development, may prove to be this something plus, which in turn will no doubt be excelled by something quite other than either of them, not yet thought of. So it is in other fields; a little gun powder, now the atomic bomb.

The jet plane appeared only in 1945, when stories of how it could fly six hundred miles an hour, or more, were taken tentatively. It was then too swift to be controlled except when flying in a straight line. No doubt it will be fully mastered. How much strain the human body can stand in such flight is part of the problem.

The same year it was announced in the House of Commons that in addition to the famous fast Meteor another jet plane was in the early stage of development, and would attain a speed of seven hundred and twenty miles an hour, which is faster than sound travels.

The Hercules, built in Culver City, California, carries wings thirteen feet thick at the hull, has a wing span of three hundred and twenty feet, and is propelled by eight motors each of three thousand horsepower.

Numbers mark these developments as well as speed. Aircraft have become as numerous as flocks of birds. It seems but yesterday that Col. Lindbergh flew to France, yet in July, 1945, the Pan American Airways estimated that soon after the war ended 233,500 passengers would fly to Europe annually, this but a small beginning of such traffic. What aviation will become in a few decades, with cheaper rates and greater speed, no man can foresee. But facts that are emerging are worth pondering.

Planes flew from London to Montreal in 1946 in fifteen

hours, and more significant an important city always before barricaded, shut in by ice for half of each year, becomes an airport open all the year. Yesterday Moscow was mysteriously distant: now by following the Arctic Circle Route, we reach it in a few hours. "San Francisco is today as near Tokyo and Berlin," says Mr. Anthony Eden, British Secretary of Foreign Affairs, at the San Francisco Conference, "as New York was to Washington one hundred years ago." He might have added that by air Transylvania is only a little time beyond Berlin. Given a plane and we can get anywhere on the planet in sixty hours, before long with improvements perhaps we can make it between sunup and sundown.

In flying over the earth we can do many things, survey oceans and continents, carry heavy loads of goods, machinery and the like, carry troops, carry horrible explosives like the atomic bombs and drop them for death and destruction. Also we can fly far away to get things. Great mineral wealth in Canada locked since time began in inaccessible wildernesses, is now made available. Mines in New Guinea can now be reached. Men charged with the world's welfare fly over the war-torn earth and the infested seas to sit in council at Teheran and Moscow, at Dumbarton Oaks and beside the Black Sea at Yalta. Mr. Eden flew the Atlantic to attend President Roosevelt's funeral. The world has been shrinking incredibly, and the end is not yet. The *Mayflower* crossed the Atlantic in sixty-five days, the *Queen Mary* in four, and soon we shall be flying it in a few hours. And our shrunken world is crisscrossed by air lanes, along which the planes of all the nations thrum over the seas, and continents, and even the poles. Our world is one world; provincialisms, geographical, political, and intellectual, are vanishing away.

And what has all this to do with Transylvania? Just this, she has become our next door neighbor. A generation ago the United States fought Spain to end an intolerable mess in Cuba. It lay at our doors. Transylvania is as near us now as Cuba was then. For the peace of Europe and the entire world we want her to live in tranquillity, normal and unoppressed, and we cherish the same wish for the peoples who live around her. Let them federate. From the Black Sea to the Adriatic, north to the Baltic, east to the mountains, and south again to the Black Sea here is one broad place where the federation of the states, together with the elimination of the dictators who work for loot, would end many ancient woes. Hungary lies in the middle of this great place, geographically pivotal. Roumania is hardly less pivotal, just south of the mountains, and Transylvania touches them both. There she lies sheltered by her mountains and only a few hours away from us, and on her treatment may hang the peace of the world. Free all her people, free the Roumanians and Saxons and Magyars in Transylvania, and let them manage their own affairs, without subjection to Bucharest, or Budapest, or Moscow, but with the good will of all of them, and the cooperation of the other states which we hope would also have their autonomy within the Danubian Federation. Make Transylvania a member of such a Federation. And then will the muffled agony of the hidden bell be heard no more through the forests!

The racial groups within Transylvania, the so-called "Nations," are intelligent peoples. Let them alone! Let them manage their own affairs: they will make a good go of it. All of them, Roumanians, Magyars, Saxons, and others live side by side, shuffled together, everybody beside everybody. They cannot be ethnically divided, for everybody is everywhere. Even if they could be collected into ethnic groups what would it matter, what would it accomplish in this air age when distances are dead? The region has been desolated by conflicts time out of mind; must they forever keep on happening? Make an end of races trying to ride each other pig-aback.

Welded together in autonomy within a Danubian Federation the Transylvanians would make a strong "nation." "Weak and fragile is the country of one tongue and one code of manners," St. Stephen, first King of Hungary, told his son nine centuries ago. One nation could be better made up of several peoples, he meant, than out of a single race. *E Pluribus Unum!* Roumania's treatment of her minority peoples is a survival of the Middle Ages. Yes, her constitution on paper is admirable enough, but her practices under it have been quite another matter. She has shown no desire for more than one tongue and one code, her own. She has baldly practiced abuses on her minorities that are the contrary of St. Stephen's design. She strives, even recently, to make all races within her borders Roumanian. "These people will become Roumanians," King Ferdinand told me. But somehow the theory does not work well.

King Stephen's policy has been fairly well followed: Hungary bent to the times. Roumania has defied the spirit of the times. St. Stephen's policy was necessary if Hungary was to survive. By contrast Roumania has constantly followed the policy of everything for the Roumanians since she attained her recent independence in 1878. We are not unaware of many problems, the vast estates of the few and the multitudes of landless people, yet on the whole the clock was not set back in Hungary compared with Roumania. The shuffling of the races went on and has now become worldwide, it continues and increases. All our nations in the Western Hemisphere are made up of migrant folk, even the Indians in the dim past came from Asia; all the nations of North and South America are multi-racial. No dictator, no nation, can stop the clock for long. In the air age migration will not cease, more men will move faster. The nation that tries to end this migration and enslave her minorities is bidding the sun to stand still in the heavens. While she may delay evolutionary processes, she cannot thwart them. The tragedy is that the nation which tries to stop the clock may start a third world war.

In God's name let all the Transylvanians mend their own affairs. Make the land beyond the forest an autonomous part of a Danubian Federation—it cannot be cried aloud too many times—let it include as many neighboring states as may be practical. At least make a beginning of such a regional federation. The plan is by no means new. Kossuth and many others have dreamed and worked for it. Dumbarton Oaks and San Francisco fostered it in worldwide inclusiveness. Give Transylvania her autonomy now.

We beg neighboring Danubian peoples to let their memories bitter and sweet trail away behind them, and looking to the future federate, the better to raise the higher values of their living. For the good of each one of these peoples, is it too much to ask? For the good of all equally is it too much to ask of each?

Our world is one world! Men talk together through the air around the world, from what we used to call the ends of the earth, discussing our mutual concernments. There must be no famine, fly the seed. There must be no plague, fly the serum. Do these things for sweet pity's sake; yes, but more than this the famine yonder threatens us. If the plague is not stopped, it may kill us here. These are our common affairs, and self-preservation is a far stronger motive than pity.

In our deepening world unity, mutual concernments compel us. Not by turning back in mock loyalties to old diversities can we go forward, but only by creating larger unities. And Transylvania in these days, let it be repeated, is only just yonder. Her welfare is ours, and so is her calamity. When Kossuth came to America a century ago she was so remote as to be almost mythical: soon by air she will be hardly further off than Nantucket is from Boston. Misgoverned she threatens our stability. Think of her in terms of the air age.

XVI

TRANSYLVANIA

THE OLD road bends past the ancient Norman Church and its shadowed burying ground. Spring has come, the orchards everywhere are in flower, the fragrance of the apple blossoms fills the air. How we remember the sheer beauty of this country side. Later in far away Chicago, when the chill wind is blowing off the Lake, we hear a street organ playing, "It's Apple Blossom Time in Normandie!" Wistful, we, who never lived in Normandie, walk on humming the plaintive tune.

Would that a tune even more plaintive could sing to us that far away, where the Carpathians stand purple in the morning light, the acacia trees are lifting high their white blossom-laden branches. Normandie was never fairer with her apple blossoms than is Transylvania garlanded with her white acacias. They are everywhere and for us have deep appeal. They are Americans.

When the Turks were finally driven out of Hungary they left incredible desolation, for great distances there was not a house, nor a man, nor even a tree. A thousand villages had disappeared. It took generations to recultivate the desert. Comparatively of recent years, about 1850, men brought the acacias from America. They have spread and thrived.

They are more than ornaments, they give life as good trees do.

"On May time every little village dons a white headdress of acacia blossoms," says John Pelenyi, "and the air is filled with their poignant fragrance; lovers meet under acacia boughs and gypsies play gay tunes for fiery dances in acacia groves. It is the acacia tree which edges the fields where long-horned silvery oxen draw the plough and men and women sing at their work. It is the acacia tree that lines the dreamy village streets where at nightfall the bells of home-bound herds chime in with the deep tones of the church bells. Hardly does a man realize that it was introduced from America."

Not only do the Transylvanians, together with all other Hungarians live under the American acacia tree, they live or once they lived under political and educational institutions as like free American institutions as the acacia trees are alike in both the countries. The acacias flowered, spreading white garlands over the land. Free institutions no less truly garlanded it. First of all, except for the Magna Carta, men lived under the oldest constitution in Europe, which gave them free representative government. Villages, towns, cities, and districts were autonomous, minding and mending their own affairs as they do in the United States. The constitutional institutions in both countries guaranteed protection for the individual.

Here is symbolism. All the peoples of Hungary, Transylvanians and the others, living under the shade of the acacias, also lived under the protection of free institutions. Acacia blossoms blooming on valley and hillside mean more than cooling shadows, blessed as these are. They mean enrichment, food for life, energy. So did Hungary's institutions.

As the beauty of these trees, so were the health giving free institutions which transformed deserts of oppression into places where men could sow and reap and live with none to make them afraid. Protected these thousand years behind one of the oldest national boundaries in all Europe, the Hungarians had constitutional law, free institutions, and independent thinking.

These privileges of freedom need constant guarding. "Eternal vigilance is the price." Not so long before the recent war certain of our American parlor radicals, drawing room folk, prattled about "what this country needs is a Hitler to direct us." Incredible, isn't it? Yet we all heard them. Then utter calamity overwhelmed the world, profoundly hurt all of it, and silenced them. Millions died that others might be free, and all of us have been brought up standing. We will keep our constitutional freedoms.

But will we extend them? This is the most vital question. Fifty nations, the largest coalition for freedom the world ever has seen, are bound together to make sure that where people want such freedom they shall have it. It will not be enough from now on for free peoples to keep their own freedoms. Liberty is never static; it advances or recedes. The world permanently can't be half slave and half free. Hungary once had freedom over a large area, lost two thirds of this area, regained part of it, and then again lost it. Transylvania had freedom, under Roumania after the First World War lost it, in 1940 regained it in part, and in 1945 lost it again by being wholly returned to Roumania, although the end is not yet. How fast the wheel of fortune spins!

International dust fills the air and it is hard to see the lovely countryside. But the homes of the people, the handsome cattle in the meadows, the ancient churches, when you add them together are Transylvania, the beloved land that lies beyond the forest. Maybe a few pictures will help us understand it.

The high gateways admitting to the enclosed yards surrounding its houses are colorful affairs. Sometimes they are heavily carved, nearly always they are painted, now and again they are enriched by a motto. One especially expresses the spirit of Transylvanian hospitality:

"Stranger, this gate is not to bar your way, but to show you where to enter, night or day."

And once having entered, you belong. You are overwhelmed by the outflowing hospitality. You are invited in all sincerity to consider yourself a member of the family. You may also be made honorary minister of the church where you preach, or honorary dean of the district.

We arrived one morning at a fine old fifteenth century church enclosed in its fortification wall built long ago against the Turks. As we crossed the church yard the bells were ringing in the belfry and oak branches had been thrust from the belfry openings, a sign of welcome. We entered the ancient interior, our feet treading the worn dull red tiles. On either side were the dark wooden pews. Rising on either side of them were the white walls with their big plain glass windows, above us the dark, time-stained, decorated wooden ceiling. Before us was the deep chancel where the men sat facing toward the middle of the church. The women sat in the nave facing the chancel. The young unmarried women were seated in a gallery at the end of the nave, the young unmarried men in another gallery at the end of the chancel, the length of the church between them. You climbed a winding stair set in the masonry and entered the high pulpit looking down on perhaps 1,200 people, including those gathered around the walls outside who could be seen through the open windows.

I was made honorary minister of the church. I asked the minister, he had been educated at Hungarian colleges and at Oxford, what he would have me do if I came to assist him. He would let me conduct the morning prayers every week-day morning at six o'clock, he answered. For more than forty years he had been the minister and he had missed only a few of these services. The good man all those years had climbed the hill every morning listening to the bells, in winter carrying his lantern. He had lighted his way into the dark unheated church, taken his lantern up the winding stair into the pulpit and placed it on the reading desk, read the Scripture lesson and offered prayer. In the winter darkness of this big interior the lanterns of the worshippers were the only light. Even in the worst storms and the most severe cold, he told me, he never had lacked a small body of attendants. In good weather many came. Early services are held daily in all the churches, this parish was not exceptional. The cultural and spiritual life of Transylvania is church-centric to a degree that we know nothing about in the United States.

I was made honorary dean of a district. Again I was told what I must do if ever I really assumed my duties. I would be expected to visit every parish in the deanery each year and preach, go over the record books and meet with the committees. It would be very interesting indeed to be the real dean of a district and come to know the fine sturdy ministers and the attractive people. If only one knew the language! If only life were longer!

The last meeting of the day had been held in the fine old church of a large town, ministers from outlying parishes taking part. One of them explained to me that as our party would be passing through his village late that night he and his wife wished me to stop and baptize their little son. Although it developed that I could not arrive until after midnight, they urged my coming and I accepted.

The long drive over the smooth road in the darkness was restful. Only the dim little carriage lanterns cast a pale light, only the friendly clopclop of the horses' hoofs broke the stillness as we dozed comfortably in the soft night air. Suddenly the carriage stopped. We had arrived. The minister, who had preceded us, was holding a lantern beside the road. A lamp shone in the nearby parsonage window. A man with a lantern was running up the hill to the church which we could see dimly. Soon the church bell was clanging, and lights began to appear in the windows of the houses. In what seemed an incredibly short time we saw many people carrying their lanterns and wending their way up the hill to the church.

In the Protestant Transylvanian churches since the Reformation the communion table has stood, not at the east end of the chancel, but at the junction of nave and chancel, which alike are filled with pews. The floors are of stone. At christenings it is the custom for the minister to take the baby on his arm, and lifting the pitcher from the communion table to pour water over him. I felt that the little boy whom I was about to baptize, taken from his warm bed after midnight, would be treated rather roughly if we followed this ancient custom, so I used a very simple service, letting the sleeping child stay in his mother's arms, making the sign of the cross on his forehead with only a little water. He did not even waken, and was carried back to the parsonage and tucked again in his cradle still sound asleep. Perhaps the strict followers of church custom wondered if he had been thoroughly baptized!

The fee usually given the minister in villages for baptisms is a live hen, so a nice little brown hen was presented to me at the communion table. I confess that for a moment I did not know what to do with her; to take her with me presented difficulties, to leave her behind might seem ungrateful. So I gave her to the baby's mother, asking that she be made the first of a flock to be acquired for the boy as he grew older. Some years after I learned that he had quite a large flock being managed toward his education. If you want to surprise your minister and be good to him when he christens your baby, give him while he is still standing at the font a nice little live brown hen!

XVII

TRANSYLVANIAN AGONY

"THE BLACKOUT on news from the Balkans is so complete that only secondhand accounts are available about what is happening in Roumania," complains *The New York Times*. And it continues, "Whatever explosive possibilities it may hold, American prestige and responsibility are directly involved."*

Since the last statement cannot be denied, what are the "explosive possibilities?" The *Times* explains, "One can assume, and it is generally hoped, to arrange eventually population transfers."†

Who "assumes" any plan so unjust, so horrible? Who "generally hopes" for it? If we can credit the news, Roumania is transferring some of the Transylvanian Saxons, or already has transferred them, to Siberia. If the reports are true, this was done in late March and April, 1945, men between sixteen years of age and fifty, and women between sixteen and forty, some seventy thousand of them out of a Transylvanian Saxon population of six hundred thousand people. Their fine farms and villages, the news tells us, are to be given to Roumanians who will be brought into Transylvania to fill their places.

* New York Times, Editorial, Feb. 27, 1945.
† New York Times, March 11, 1945.

Had the Transylvanian Saxons made themselves more obnoxious to their Russian conquerors than had the Roumanians? Probably not. They had fought against Russia, as had the Roumanians until the clock of victory was striking Allied Victory, but the explanation is not to be found among the rewards and punishments. The Saxons were desirable, moveable, "expendable" and Siberia needs sturdy peoples for her development. Roumania wanted the Saxon wealth in Transylvania, farms and villages: Russia wanted the people. Their fate had nothing to do with their part in the war; they will probably be doomed to forms of slavery in mine and forest.

They were not recent arrivals from Germany.* They came to Transylvania in the twelfth century, with autonomous rights guaranteed them by the Hungarian King, rights which they enjoyed until recent years. For twenty-five years past they have tried to work with the Roumanians, none too successfully. After King Carol of Roumania called in the German troops, the Saxon Transylvanians had to bend to the Germans. True, they fought against Russia, but so did the Roumanians who are said to be receiving their farms and villages. The motivation for this policy of deportation is plain. Russia wants the Transylvanian Saxons for what they are. Roumania wants all they leave behind, and she wants to settle Roumanians on their land. Were any of the United Nations consulted? Says the *Times*, "American prestige and responsibility are involved."

We are set thinking on long lines. What gives a racial group the right to continue to live in the territory it occupies? Felling the forest, clearing the land, taming the desert; then residence over a reasonable period, the ability and

* For Account of Transylvanian Saxons, see Appendix 3.

willingness to work the region's resources, agricultural and other, its defense when attacked, its schools and colleges and all other institutions founded and maintained for the common good, these are among the constructive qualifications for group citizenship in every territory. And the Transylvanian races have stood these tests for centuries. All of them arrived in Transylvania twice as long ago as the Pilgrims came to Plymouth, Massachusetts. All are old residents who together have built up that precious entity, a real regional community consciousness.

We must make this clear. The Magyars arrived in the Plain under Prince Arpad about 895. One or more of their tribes early trekked up the valleys, and penetrated through the forest to the land that lies beyond. But there their position was insecure. War-like peoples lived on the other side of the mountains to the east and south. The Hungarian King Stephen (1000–1038) saw the danger, and sent his armies successfully against Gyula's tribe at Gyulafehervar. Thus he protected his eastern lands from the Bessenyos, distant kinsmen of the Magyars, living in what is now Roumania. Later other inroads brought the Hungarian King Laszlo (1077–1095) into Transylvania, where he successfully fought his enemies.

The Szekelys claim to have arrived a century before the Magyars, to whom they were akin, settling in the bend of the Carpathians. A free yeomanry, they held their lands in common, paid no taxes, and became the most democratic of the three groups. Some of their privileges they kept until recent days. To them and to the Saxons was largely left the defense of the eastern border.

King Matthias was dealing with them in the last half of

the fifteenth century, and his court historian, Bonfinius, comments, "The Szekelys cannot endure servitude, and they worship liberty to such a degree that they would rather die than pay taxes."* To be taxed, since only the serfs bore taxation, was a mark of servitude. They gave military service. Their spirit finds expression in an old Szekely saying, "I recognize no superiors—but also no subordinates." Always they have been a sturdy and outstanding people.

The Roumanians claim to have descended from the Dacians, and so to be the earliest of the early settlers, a debated contention on which we cannot enter in our limited space. All authorities agree that whenever it was that they first came in appreciable numbers, more Roumanians followed them, fleeing from the Turks and the tyranny of their own rulers, and seeking the safety of the mountains. All agree that they have been there for a long time, great numbers having come in the late seventeenth and eighteenth centuries. Indeed, they arrived in such numbers that in time they formed a racial group larger than the original Magyar population.

In passing it may be helpful for Americans to remember that in recent years immigration to the United States has been restricted in order to prevent the same thing happening here.

The Roumanians were the last of the races resident in Transylvania to express their national or racial consciousness. It was not until the end of the eighteenth century (1790–'91), that they formulated plans to secure equal rights with the Saxons. Unfortunately the times were not favorable to recognizing more autonomous units within the

* "The Szekelys," Benedict de Janesó, p. 29.

state. The French Revolution (1789) had spread abroad the larger conception of a unified state wherein all citizens should be free and equal. Even Kossuth in the middle of the nineteenth century opposed granting autonomous rights to the Roumanians, not because of any antagonism to them, but because autonomous racial rights within the state had become antiquated by comparison with one common citizenship and the same freedom for all.

We turn again to the Saxons, the last of the Transylvanian races to arrive, coming in the middle of the twelfth century. King Bela III of Hungary (1173–1196), following the policy of his predecessors to protect his borders, settled them in the region between the Olt and the Maros, then uninhabited and covered with forests, and gave them rights which they continued to enjoy until recent years. They have borne the brunt of many conflicts, they have proved themselves able and industrious, a people of intelligence and high standards. They were not Nazi. Now, if the news can be trusted, some of these Saxons have become candidates for deportation to Siberia, and something less than seventy thousand of them are reported to have been deported. The news astounds and distresses the United Nations; it is important that we understand what it means to the territory as a whole.

The races of Transylvania have slowly built a precious regionalism, the foundation on which every state must stand if it is to have permanence and security. Regionalism, a common regional consciousness, is of slow growth, to possess it is an achievement. In Transylvania, if the reports are true, it is about to be broken by this dire transfer of population.

To focus the facts it is essential that we understand this

regionalism. Says Count Aponyi, "The Hungarian nation includes a sub-nation; the Transylvanian nation, which forms a natural geographic section: with a history of its own. This Transylvanian sub-nation is not a fiction; it is a strong living reality. It consists of Magyars (918,000 or 43%), Saxons (234,000 or 8.7%), and Roumanians (1,-472,000 or 55%), the rest miscellaneous.* Whose stamp does it (Transylvania) bear? Not necessarily that of the most numerous race; but of those races which have stood foremost in the Transylvanian life-work, political, cultural, and economic, which shaped the whole mass into a national unit. It has been done almost exclusively by the Magyars and Saxons. Together they represented 79.6% of the intellectuals, 74.8% of the townspeople, 67.8% of the leaders in economic life. The Roumanians are slowly coming to the front; until lately they had no conspicuous part in the national life. From their mass only a comparatively small—though constantly increasing—number have risen to the higher walks of life, as priests, teachers, and lawyers. The Transylvanian sub-nation grants equal rights and equal chances to all its component races; but leadership cannot be determined by violence, nor by legal fiction, nor by rough numbers; it is attained only by preeminence in every branch of national activity."

Count Aponyi at the peace table after the First World War asked "for the constitution of Transylvania as a separate state." He wanted its regionalism preserved. Says Macartney, "If the problem of the middle Danube Basin is ever to be achieved, a complete reorientation of ideas is

---

* "Pictures of Transylvania," Count Aponyi. The author is not responsible for incompatability in the figures, and leaves them as published in 1904. No doubt proportionally they were correct.

necessary. The oppression of one nationality by another can never bear any good fruit. The ideal of the future must be cooperation between equals."*

It is hard in these days to see clearly, to understand, to give praise where it is due. We are profoundly grateful to Russia for protecting the world against Germany. For two years she alone fought, for two terrific years she stayed the German armies and then flung them back. True, she had equipment sent her, sixteen thousand tanks from the United States is a single item, but it was the men of Russia who fought and died and defeated the Germans. At the start England stood alone, heroically, magnificently; then Russia took on. Dull should we be indeed and ungrateful if we did not pay tribute to England and to Russia where it is due.

All this on the one hand, but on the other why should Russia give this terrible punishment to some of the Saxons of Transylvania? True, Russia endured a great upheaval; but the aim of the Soviet, it is claimed, is the good of the great masses of the people. Vast sums of money like those once spent by the Czar and his nobles upon themselves have of late years been spent to transform Russia, to give her industries and technical education. In short we remember how widespread has been the awakening. Now great projects are going forward, and among them is the settlement of Siberia, which needs people like the Saxons. But our hearts cry out. Why should Russia consent and Roumania execute such a cruel plan as deporting Transylvanian Saxons, whose people tamed the desert and felled the forests and have lived on their lands these past seven centuries?

It is high time that we in the United States learned to see

* C. A. Macartney, "Hungary," p. 332.

colors clearly and not confuse them, not be color blind. Because we are grateful to Russia for her part in the Second World War is no reason, if the reports are true, why we should not make every inquiry about the alleged deportations. If the aim of the Soviet Government, as we are told, is the good of the masses of the people, why not of other peoples beside the Russians? How is it that these sturdy and intelligent Saxons who love their Transylvanian homeland and have loved it for these past seven centuries are to be sent into permanent exile? We do not know where they will be placed, or to what fate they will be doomed; but it is time the world cried out. We protest, with all our might we protest!

The stench of the whole procedure rises to high heaven. The Nazis practiced it. Three million Poles were "transferred," some to slave labor in Germany, others through Russia to Siberia. Several million Jews were deported, and with the greatest cruelty. French people who had lived for generations in Alsace were driven into France, and to slave labor in Germany. There is not a race in Central Europe today that is not in terror of deportation if and when the evil days shall come. Is this barbarous treatment of minorities to continue? Is it to become an international habit to make use of deportation, throwing over its horrors the thin disguise of political expediency? Is this to be the triumph of democracy?

The high cost of deportation in human suffering, and death, and waste is ghastly, appalling beyond computing, beyond imagining. Exact figures of mass deportations and the following enslavements are unavailable, but it cannot be denied that there is more slave labor in the world today than ever there was before. And in these hideous affairs "The prestige and responsibility of the United States are involved," as are those of all the United Nations.

Consider what mass deportations mean. Thousands, even millions of men and women, the overwhelming proportion of them hopelessly separated from their families, the old and the sick, little children and women with child, have trudged weary miles, or like cattle have been packed into box cars where they have been unable to sit down or recline, and have been endlessly shunted about, before at last many of them had the good fortune to die and be thrown down by the roadside. "Transfers" of population mean heartbreak, and agony, and death: let it be cried from the housetops of the world that this is one of the blackest crimes in all the long record of human woe.

XVIII

DANUBIAN FEDERATION

THE BIG meeting had ended. The ancient Transylvanian church with its bare white interior was empty. I stood alone for a little on the terrace, looking out across the wide cultivated fields. Below the terrace I saw a stalwart woman walking toward me, her bare feet treading softly in the dust of the road. She mounted the steps, slowly approached me smiling, put down her heavy load, and sociably resting her arms on the railing said to me in excellent English, "It is a lovely country, isn't it?"

She enjoyed my surprise at her speaking English. In many gatherings people spoke to me in my own tongue. My new friend, it appeared, had made several trips across the ocean to Pittsburgh, Pennsylvania, where she had worked in the mills until she had accumulated a little capital to bring back to her beloved village. She was slowly buying a small house and the bit of land around it. Yonder I could see the red tiled roof above the trees as she pointed it out to me. She was approaching middle age, born of the very countryside, beautiful in her abundant strength. She belonged in the deep way that a traveller never attains. She had belonged ever since Arpad and his followers arrived in 895; she was a fine representative of the sturdy Magyars.

I put beyond her any but the most friendly intentions in her voyagings; but I could not help reflecting that if ever centuries before in some previous incarnation she had leapt upon her horse and gone raiding, how magnificently she must have done it! There is great power in the Magyars. You feel their reserve strength. "These people," King Ferdinand had said to me, "will become Roumanians." Well, maybe! But it will be a very long time hence; perhaps not until the mouth of hell shall freeze.

The friendly woman typified migratory labor. Why, indeed, should labor be immobile? In the United States we are familiar with the roving harvesters who move about the country doing seasonal work. Before the acute immigration problems following the First World War seasonal workers came from Europe and returned. We used to see them on the Atlantic steamers going to and fro happily enough. I had said to the woman, "Bye and bye you will stay in America?" "No, no," she had answered, "I come home." Some like her journeyed back and forth. Fortunately for the United States, many Magyars stayed. Between 1900 and 1910, 210,000 came annually from Austria-Hungary to make the United States their permanent home, perhaps half of them Magyars. At a Milwaukee dinner I found eleven men from Hungary, of whom four were Transylvanians, all now American citizens, all doing well. This was not unique.

Freedom to take to the roads of the world and seek the greener fields has been fought for, lost and won since history began; fundamentally it is a labor problem, forever pressing, forever difficult, but not insoluble. Into its intricacies we cannot enter, but woe to the government which blocks the open roads! With the world one place, with transportation available to the ends of the earth, and its facilities ever increasing, labor must be free to seek its own. There can be no serfdom, men tied to the land, in the Utopia we are so slowly building.

The European states, before as well as following World War I, erected barriers around themselves, customs, quotas, exchanges, and the rest. Banking up of populations inside the countries resulted in all sorts of maladjustments, including much unemployment, which could have been eased if not ended had the workers been allowed to move about.

This banking up of the population has been disastrous. "Europe was caught in a tangle of administrative controls over trade and finance," says Professor Condliffe,* "and this tangle gave the totalitarians their opportunity. They climbed into power on the backs of the unemployed. Once in power they found the regimented centralized trade controls a most effective instrument of power policy. The Second World War began on this front and within a few years Germany dominated, not only the trade, but the internal economic policies of most Central and Eastern European countries. Once Austria was occupied, the way was clear for pressure on the Czechs, for Berchtesgaden, Godesberg, Munich, the occupation of Prague, and the Second World War. Between 1933 and 1939 Germany had softened up her prospective victims, mainly under cover of economic negotiations. The main conclusion has gained new importance. The backward economic development of Eastern Europe is a constant source of political weakness, and therefore a con-

* Prof. J. B. Condliffe, University of California, "The Danube Basin and the German Economic Sphere," p. ix.

stant temptation to aggressive industrial power. Industrial development of this great region is one of the keys to a solution of Europe's perpetual feuds."* (abbreviated)

Says Antonin Basch, "Germany's dream had neared fulfillment. Southeastern Europe was rapidly becoming a part of the German economic empire. She had become master of the entire area, a German domination surpassing in ruthlessness and thoroughness the German and Austro-Hungarian rule before 1914."*

Looking at Germany's all but complete economic penetration and control of her neighbors in the years just before the war, we marvel that nothing was done to stop her. But who was big and strong enough? Not the little states, nor any one or two of them, not any one big power who would have brought the wrath of Germany upon herself. Meanwhile Germany's grip tightened. Every road leads to Rome! Every international problem leads back to the need of world federation. The chief hope of the United Nations in permanent Union is that together they will become a power big and strong enough to check inimical trends and policies while they are still modest affairs, not gigantic evils sprawling over half a continent. The same considerations apply to our international situation. Certain aspects of them demand attention.

Prompt action is essential to the solution of these problems. It is a colossal mistake, and it may yet bring disaster, to believe that problems hard to solve now will be solved later on by some gradual and magical evolution. The very contrary is true. Every war creates fluid conditions, history proves it, but they last only for brief periods. Wars upset old customs, destroy half dead institutions, shatter old be-

* Antonin Basch, "Danube Basin and German Economic Sphere," p. 1.

liefs. But life has to go on. Either it creates new forms, new institutions, or else for want of them it sinks back into the old.

If ever the history of men can be written in a few broad surveys the historian will record this strangest of all human phenomena, the quick return of life to its old channels even after the greatest of upheavals. Following the First World War when men had worked mightily to dig new channels, once peace came they rested. We all felt the world weariness. Some historians charge us with international laziness. It cannot be denied that insufficient attention was given to the international follow-up work which was absolutely essential if the advantages of victory were to become permanent.

The writer of this book at the time was speaking over the country where he could get a hearing on the needs of Transylvania. Like many other speakers questing for their causes, of course he met much apathy, often called war weariness or international laziness, bad names applied to good people. One reason for it was that we had no implements! Tell the man to dig up the garden, but give him no shovel! There was the League of Nations, which we Americans deserted and ever after found fault with. It proved weak, a poor stick to lean on. All this is of the past, except that it points the importance of the United Nations Organization, and encourages us to believe that the United States and the some fifty other nations associated for making peace and guarding it in the future can cure incipient regional diseases more easily before they become epidemic. Model your figure while the clay is pliable; if it hardens you will have to use an axe. Now, not later, is the time to solve intricate international problems.

The great region we are pleading for, including Transylvania, stretches from the Baltic on the North to the Adriatic and the Black Seas on the South, from Russia on the East into Germany on the West, and comprises states containing perhaps a quarter of the population of Europe. It is without natural defenses like the Carpathians. To dissociate its component parts has been the game of its powerful neighbors, who have sought to increase its diversities and then to rule at least parts of it. The broad roadway of the Orient into Europe, it has witnessed invasions without number. Perhaps it has been ravaged by more wars than any other equal area on the planet. Its many states lie edge to edge like pieces of a jigsaw puzzle and in the main are defenseless. Suppose this region could be united and then allowed to develop its own self-sustaining economy?

Suppose left to themselves to work out their salvation all these people could associate permanently, a hundred million of them, state with state, for defense and development. Ponder the fact that air armadas will determine future political or governmental combinations, and the accompanying fact that even now only the largest and richest states can afford them.* Within a few decades no one nation alone may be able to afford them. The permanent organization of the United Nations for peace and world cooperation, it is hoped, will take the smaller nations literally under its wings. Heaven send the day! But until it dawns would it not be wise for the nations of Eastern Europe to associate at least for self defense?

The Germans probably will become one of the great peoples of the future. The world wants them to be, provided they become men of peace; only so can other men live. But will a sometime restored Germany remain at

* See Propulsion, Chap. XV.

peace? Who can tell? Our region lies next to Germany, and it well might have defense ready in time of need. Had the region been coordinated twenty-five years ago, had it possessed real defensive power, Europe then and again since 1939 might have seen different days. This is no more than speculation except as it points to the life-saving advantage of this whole political Central European diversity transforming itself into unity and speaking with one voice.

On the east of our region lies Russia, as Germany lies on her west. It would be an advantage to her if Central Europe could be federated. She is herself "a Union of Soviet Republics." She could deal better with one federated Mid-European state than with many. Doubtless her attitude would be determined by the form such federation would take, and meanwhile we do not forget our gratitude to Russia for the marvelous role she played in stopping the Germans on their road to world dominance. What Western civilization owes her cannot be reckoned.

It is extraordinary how little talk of federation in Eastern Europe appears in our press,* which seems mostly to speculate about who among the old established states will get the pieces. This may be due to the silence of the whole region. It could hardly have been speaking in the recent chaos, true; but plans for federation in this time of disassociation seem hardly more substantial than the myriad glow worms hovering over the nearby meadow at night, faint lights moving without direction. This may be because diversity cannot speak articulately. When the region speaks now it only argues or as in the past, fights.

Examine this consideration. From the general silence about the advantages of regional federations as progressive

* See "Hope for United States of Europe," *Saturday Evening Post*, April 7, 1945.

steps toward world federation, it would seem that all the little nations are expected silently and humbly to troop along into whatever the main world federation shall become. Excellent so far as it goes, this is not enough to secure lasting peace.

In Eastern Europe the small nations themselves must learn the art of union, call such combinations by whatever name we please, and there are encouraging signs.* Speaking together, what a tremendous influence they could wield! The states united in our American Union, our United States, carry immensely more weight internationally when speaking with one voice than they would if each of them only recorded its own opinion. One out of many!*

"The security of these peoples (of the Danube Basin)," says C. A. Macartney,* "depends on whether such healthy conditions can be created between them that they will continue to defend themselves and each other ... (p. 153 ibid.). Association for common defense, a degree of common foreign policy is indispensable for security."

He enumerates the nations.† "Of the peoples usually reckoned as Danubian," he says,

The Roumanians number	14	million
Magyars	12	"
Czechs	7½	"
Serbs	7	"
Bulgars	5½	"
Croats	3½	"
Slovaks	2½	"
Slovenes	1	"

* "Problems of the Danube Basin," p. 151.
† See Chapter "Who Wants Federation?"

He continues his list. On either flank of them living under conditions hardly to be distinguished from theirs, are

Poles	20	million
Turks	12	"
Greeks	6	"

And then he gives the names only, no numbers, of the Finns, Lithuanians, Letts, Estonians, and Albanians.

He admits that his list is incomplete. "This statement ignores a vast number of half differentiated peoples . . . Keansen and Hazuls, Ugro-Rusins and Bipovans, Crisani and Karakachans, Mirdites, and Wends, Bunyevci, Csangos and Sokei, and heaven knows what besides."

All these peoples of the Basin, and those others near it, through the centuries have been churned together. "None of them," says Macartney, "forms the only ethnic element even in the heart of its chief home: fragments of other nationalities are dotted like islands in its sea, and conversely outlying fragments of its own nationality dot the homes of its neighbors."*

The region converges to the Danube, which flows through it for 1750 miles, passing near the center of the settlements of eleven major peoples, among whom there live shuffled indiscriminately no less than twenty-six peoples in all. Viewed historically the region has been the road from the East to the West, and from West to East, for hordes of migrant peoples and for armies trying to thwart them or themselves bent on conquest. The great river on its way to the sea, says Macartney, "has passed the enormous Hungarian plain with its wheat and maize, its sunflowers and

* "Problems of the Danubian Basin," p. 4.

acacias, and its long-horned shamble-footed white oxen churning dust the color of their own hides out of the rutted paths."

One long panorama of smiling lands and busy peoples, the great river empties at last into the sea. If world peace is to be built, man's greatest achievement, this whole vast region converging on the Danube cannot be ignored. Either the region must be included, "harmonized," or there will be another war or wars.

But how difficult it is to try thinking of harmonizing perhaps a hundred million people, or maybe more. We need guidance, and a guide is at hand, in the person of Count Paul Teleki, Hungarian Prime Minister. He had been working on plans for Danubian Federation, and the night that was to end all his hopes was falling. In those dark days of 1941 he was under the espionage of the German gestapo, there were a thousand of their agents in Budapest known to the Hungarian police, yet he managed to receive an intimate friend very late at night, and through him he sent the following information to his friends in the United States.*

He foresaw clearly the complete defeat of Nazi Germany, and the European chaos that would result from the war. He believed that no future was conceivable for any of the minor nations in eastern and central Europe if they tried to continue to live their isolated national lives. He asked his friends in America to help them establish a federal system, to federate. This alone could secure for them the two major assets of national life; first, political and military security, and, second, economic prosperity. Hungary, he emphasized, stood ready to join in such collaboration, pro-

* So far as the author can learn it has not been published before.

vided it was firmly based on the complete equality of all the member states.

To the question, which nations could usefully federate, he gave two answers. A minimum federation would considerably improve conditions. It would be within the strategic triangle of Europe formed by Budapest, Vienna and Prague. It would combine those nations living in the Carpathian Basin formed by the Carpathian and Sudeten mountains and the Alps. It is a dire mistake, he held, to believe that the peace of Europe can be defended on the Rhine. The Danube, not the Rhine, is the European river. Only by solving the Danubian problem can the peace of Europe be established.

Desirable as Teleki believed this minimum union to be, he favored a larger federation. Besides the nations just mentioned (Hungary including autonomous Transylvania, Austria and Czechoslavakia), he believed all the Balkan nations could be wisely joined. He did not fear lowering the Danubian higher price level, wage level, social standards, etc., by allowing unhampered Balkan competition. He pointed out that the Balkan peoples—Yugoslavs, Roumanians, Bulgarians, Albanians and Greeks—have made great and rapid progress since their comparatively recent liberation from Turkish domination. They have developed an intelligent and progressive middle class, intensified their agricultural production, and started successful industrialization. While elimination of all tariff barriers within the proposed federation, Teleki agreed, would involve readjustments and temporary losses, these would be soon compensated by free access to raw materials and a far larger market.

The greatest, the most important advantage to the member states in the larger federation, in Teleki's view, would be their greater security. They would then enjoy in Europe a standing equal with the great powers and they could successfully resist undesirable interferences and intrigues from outside, which in the past have made life intolerable throughout this whole Danubian region. The young nations would be free to develop their energies and talents. The region would show the quickest development in all Europe.

This is important testimony. Let its appearance here be also our heartfelt tribute to a great European statesman.

But again to go back to our beginning, we wonder what happened to the Magyar woman who stood beside me on the terrace by the church. Did she voyage over and back again before chaos came and finish buying her little house and bit of land? Is it still hers or has somebody taken it away from her? Village and regional and national governments mean freedom to move about, and not be shut in, and security. "The little house says stay! And the little road says go!" We must be free to do both. What will keep the roads of Eastern Europe open so men can walk in peace? Federation, association, union, getting together for the common good.

"This war has shown that small nations in an era of mechanized warfare are unable to defend themselves," says Edward R. Stettinius, Jr., formerly United States Secretary of State. "Only the great powers possess the industrial capacity and other military resources required to defeat aggressors." FEDERATION!!!

"The Assembly will have an effective instrument in building peace," our ex-Secretary of State continues. "The Economic and Social Council is provided for in recognition of a great fact which increasingly characterizes international life. The whole world is more and more one single area of interdependent technological inventions, industrial methods, marketing problems and their related social effects. Either universal economic friction will disrupt the world toward war or universal economic cooperation will harmonize the world toward peace. The Council is to promote respect for human rights and fundamental freedoms."

"The (Dumbarton Oaks) plan takes into account both the world's stubborn realities and the world's unquenchable aspirations."*

Our area has three natural groupings; the Polish-Baltic, the Danubian, and the Balkan, and these for geo-political reasons. The Bohemian watershed should divide the region from Germany. The Danubian group could contain no less than Austrians, Czechs, Hungarians and Transylvanians and Slovaks. For the protection of the entire Danubian grouping, as well as for her own sake, Transylvania should become an autonomous part of it. Croatia, Serbia, and Roumania, while not as vital to the Danubian as they would be to the Balkan group, in the writer's considered opinion, would greatly strengthen it. "The three groups would be bound together by a common concern for their joint defense, embodied in a close agreement for defense and in a preferential arrangement for inter-regional trade."

Here is a definite plan for federation, growing out of the fertile soil of common concernments. Each constituent region, it will be observed, would preserve a maximum independency and identity, within the federation. Looking down the years ahead of us, while the rest of the world is federating, this region should be federating.

* Abbreviated from "What the Dumbarton Oaks Peace Plan Means," by Edward R. Stettinius, Jr., The Reader's Digest, February 1945.

Take note of the world tendency to federate. The present states of Europe are all combinations of earlier little independencies. Spain, Italy, and France, Germany, Russia. and Great Britain, and the others, are combinations of small regional groupings which lost their significance and merged as the world shrank. The Dominion of Canada, a spacious name like the great land it describes, and Commonwealth of Australia, a whole continent, only became political unities late in the last century, within the frame of the British Empire. Our United States is another example. It was to save the thirteen little struggling American States that Madison and Hamilton and Jay held out for a federal government. The unities of science, and the rest, promote the getting together of men. Great Britain before World War II offered to federate with France.*

"World Federation is in the air." The saying goes back to the merging of little South American groups into nations which freed themselves from Spain, in the early nineteenth century. It is far more literally true now than it was then. Aircraft fly about the nations busily gossiping; the world is one, and not so big after all. The League of Nations, and the United Nations are logical steps in global development. Certain regions may hang back, may delay progress toward world unity and peace; but in the end regional resistance will prove weaker than the global participation.

There is nothing new in the plan for Danubian federation. Kossuth has been named its originator. He wanted constitutional freedom for Hungary, including Transylvania, then an Austrian province, freedom with constitutional guarantees, and he demanded the same guarantees

* See Appendix 2 for the "Draft of Union" presented to France by Great Britain.

of constitutional government for all the other states of the great Austrian Empire. Somewhat later he wanted federation of the surrounding countries.† Later still he wanted Britain and the United States to form a union, at least for certain purposes.

Exact priority in urging such federation is neither easy to prove, nor is it particularly important. But it is important to remember that Kossuth, great champion of human liberty, who gave his life to furthering constitutionality and to the hope of mid-European federation, came to believe that this was the only cure for the endless quarrels of Central Europe. Few men ever have had the right to speak which was his, bought by a lifetime of work and suffering. Again, except through Danubian federation, he held that there was no solution, no hope.

It is curious to note how often the teaching of imperative necessity quite literally comes line upon line, precept upon precept, here a little and there a little, until it is accepted, until at last it prevails. During the century since Kossuth, the hope of Danubian federation has burned and smouldered and burned again. The peacemakers of Versailles are reproached today because they did not make some form of Danubian federation mandatory. "The main political principle upon which Versailles constructed a new order was the only one possible; the national liberty and independence of the small peoples. The mistakes may lie in the fact that these small peoples of Central Europe were not *authoritatively advised* to set up a cooperation which would provide them with the advantages of a great commonwealth able to normalize and stabilize its relations with its neighbors, and therefore able to be a strong factor for peace and

† When in England he tried to start a Danubian federation.

security. . . ." This is the most promising alternative before the world's peacemakers, and it would solve the Transylvanian problem. For this plan we are begging consideration.

Milan Hodža, whom we quote, leader of the Slovak Peasant Party, was Prime Minister of Czechoslovakia from 1935 to 1938. "A federalized Central Europe," he says, "is one of the absolute necessities of a postwar peace. It is the only organism possible for making use of the national forces which in that region can preserve the principle of national and individual liberty and ordered freedom, and can join a reasonable system of production and consumption and market policy upon which a new Europe is to follow. If there is a new Europe to follow, it is neither prepared nor able to renounce a hundred million freedom-loving people and a hundred million possible consumers."

The common good requires "Central Europe to be not a mosaic of several weak states, but a federation of them all. . . . How essentially different the European outlook might have been in 1914 if the Danube Valley had housed not a group of oppressed nations, but a Commonwealth of free ones. . . . Germany's task to set up fair relations with her neighbors will be facilitated by putting the small nations on an equal footing with her. That, however, means federation. . . . In cooperation only lies security."

Why has not some form of Danubian federation come long since? Because every time there has been a real chance one or another of the great powers has blocked it. The vetoing power would have to give up something and refuses.

An example already mentioned is Macedonia. Ever since the Turks were driven out in 1912 her problem has been threatening the peace of Europe. Only federation can solve it, in which the Serbs and Bulgarians must figure equally as independent units and Macedonia be an equal member. On October 2, 1944, an agreement was signed by Marshal Tito, representing Yugoslavia, and by the Bulgarian Government. Both powers recognized the necessity of federation, and Russia fully backed the plan. The Macedonians would gladly have accepted it, they always have stood for unity and autonomy. But the British Government, in March, 1945, vetoed the inclusion of Bulgaria. Evidently she feared that such a Yugoslav federation would upset the balance of power in the Balkans, and endanger the British position in Greece, vital to her Mediterranean life line. Experts disagree on the problems involved. One party sees more strength in federation; the other, mindful of the terrific responsibilities she carries, aware of the danger she lives in, fears that federation would increase them. Both parties seek some stronger stability.

Precisely the same sort of complexity has always stopped progress toward Danubian federation. Transylvania has been left in exactly the same position regarding it that Macedonia occupied in regard to the proposed Yugoslav federation. A big power dissents, the plan becomes impractical, a chance to further peace slips by.

Another question. What will be Russia's final attitude on Danubian federation, including autonomy for Transylvania? In March, 1945, Moscow stated that the decision must await the reestablishment of the regular governments. This would be more reassuring if we had the facts about the deportation of the Saxons from Transylvania to Siberia.

Without yielding any part of our purpose of federation, and its urgency, it will require unlimited patience and planning perhaps through several generations, we must be slow in passing judgment on each situation. It is easy enough for us to be impatient and critical for we carry no responsibility. Hesitation on the part of the great powers to encourage regional federations comes mainly from caution. Shall they scrap such fixity as exists for cooperative plans which however excellent are as yet untried? And this while they are laboring on the greatest international cooperation men ever have dreamed of? The organization of the United Nations for peace must bring them reasonable certainty of international stability. Only then can they run the risks of encouraging regional federations freely. With reasonable assurance of world stability the problems involved will become less formidable. Meantime we can urge the fullest consideration of every opportunity and try to create a world wide will toward collaboration.

Federation is a mighty incoming tide in the affairs of men. It will yet float our ships of state from off the shoals.

XIX

WHO WANTS DANUBIAN AUTONOMY AND FEDERATION?

THE PEOPLE living in Transylvania want autonomy and federation. We take the three groups, or "nations" separately.

The Transylvanian Roumanians expected something like autonomy at the end of the First World War. Austria and Hungary had signed an armistice, November 5, 1918. No enemy soldiers were then on Hungarian soil; but her enemies had occupied two thirds of her lands by the time of the Peace Treaty, and a year and a half earlier these same lands had been incorporated into foreign states. The Peace Treaty twenty-five years ago did no more than recognize or legalize existing conditions. Transylvania had been occupied by Roumanian armies. Under such conditions the long resident Roumanians began to take over. At first they wanted autonomy or something very like it; later when disappointed they expected a rule at least equivalently good to that they had had from Budapest. Looking ahead they were glad that Transylvania was to be part of Great Roumania.

But the intervening quarter century has brought them

continuing disillusionment. Now they have turned bitter, but why? They have watched the decay of moral standards, and the prevailing inefficiency in things small and large. The streets have been left unmended, railroad coaches are left uncleaned and their windows broken, general shabbiness deteriorates into wreckage. Far more vital are the larger matters, constant looting by the police, collection of heavy taxes arbitrarily imposed, and allegedly disappearing to Bucharest. There is little evidence of their being spent on the needs of Transylvania. The long resident Roumanians resent the incredible intrusion of practices usually associated with the Orient in their Transylvanian homeland where before they were unknown.* The Transylvanian Roumanians want autonomy. They gave good evidence of it after the First World War, deeds worth remembering. At the end of 1918 their leaders held a meeting at Gyulafehervar, where they passed significant resolutions. We quote only those witnessing the essential togetherness of the three Transylvanian peoples, and expressing that regional consciousness already mentioned:

"III. 1. Complete national (racial) liberty for all peoples.

"2. All religious beliefs shall have equal rights and full religious autonomy shall prevail.

"3. True democracy to be established in all domains of the public life.

"4. Full freedom of the press and right of assembly; free propagation of human thought."†

At the meeting in Gyualafehervar the leaders chose a Governing Council to sit at Nagyszeben and administer Transylvania.

* See Panariote system, Chap. XIV.
† Andrew Rónai, translated from "Transylvania," Budapest, 1940.

But in these judicious plans the Roumanian Transylvanians were doomed to disappointment, for no sooner had the Peace Conference fixed the new frontiers than the Bucharest Government dissolved the Governing Council and took over all powers. Says Rónai, "The Gyulafehervar resolution went by the board, and Transylvania never got its autonomy." The Transylvanian Roumanians wanted autonomy in 1918: they want it now.

To this end in the early twenties the Peasant Party (Taranist), their strongest political group, put a plank in their platform that Transylvania must become autonomous within Great Roumania. Throughout the succeeding years this policy has been constantly advocated by Julius Maniu, himself a Roumanian Transylvanian, a truly democratic leader and Roumanian patriot, a man of marked ability and sterling character who never has surrendered to the corruption around him. At his personal peril he fought Nazism in Roumania. The Transylvanian Roumanians want autonomy because their government would then be far better than that which has existed in recent years. It might later prove to be a step toward Danubian federation and Transylvanian autonomy within it.

The second Transylvanian group, the Saxons, have long favored an autonomous Transylvania and for the same reasons.* No doubt they would loyally accept and support it under Roumania if given the chance. Reports of their deportation to Siberia are not complete.†

The third group, the Transylvanian Magyars and the Szekelys, have long wanted as much regional independence as they could get. Kossuth's demand on Austria, that Tran-

* See Chapter XVII.
† For a full account of the Saxons see Appendix 3.

sylvania be returned to Hungary, doubtless contemplated recognition of regional needs in Transylvania as distinct from those of the Hungarian Plain. He wanted to bring Transylvania back to Hungary "as a child to its mother's arms." Certain it is that after the Austrian Hungarian Union of 1867 there was an undercurrent of dissatisfaction with the insufficient attention that Budapest gave to Transylvania down to the end of the First World War.

During these past eighty odd years this desire for autonomy has been cherished in one form or another by the Szekelys and Transylvanian Magyars. It is nothing new. Regional needs demand regional government. Doubtless the Transylvanian Magyars and Szekelys would prefer autonomy within a Danubian federation to autonomy within Great Roumania; but also Great Roumania to the misrule they have long endured from Bucharest.

Julius Maniu, leader of the Peasant Party in Transylvania and all Roumania, does not battle alone. A word of explanation, "peasant" is unfamiliar in our American vocabulary: we are likely to think of a peasant as a man with a hoe; but the party name really means no more than "democratic," a party of the people. It includes all classes. Maniu's plans for Transylvanian autonomy have the support of Peasant Parties in adjoining countries, including of course their own needs. Both Roumanian and Hungarian* Peasant Parties have been in constant touch with the Peasant Parties in Croatia, Slovakia, Austria, Poland and Serbia. The identity of their views and purposes has been formerly expressed. These leaders and their followers are important for the future of Danubian Federation; they

* In Hungary called the Small Holders' Party, in reference to farms as contrasted with the great estates.

may yet control their governments and be able to lead, and meanwhile they are addressing themselves to the world. In the future world parliament the United Nations will hear from them.

At the Peasant Party International Congresses, largely initiated by F. Milan Hodža, Prime Minister of Czechoslovakia and leader of the Slovak Peasant Party, demand has been made for the federation of all Europe as the only way to lasting peace. In urging European Confederation they have supporting Count Coudenheve-Calergi's Pan-European organization.* Many Transylvania members of other parties support Danubian federation.

Hungary has stood ready to join a federation, including an autonomous Transylvania, provided it was based on complete equality of the member nations. This should be recognized because several neighbor states, including Hungary, have been blamed for not responding to overtures from the Little Entente, which in reality looked to the dominance of the Entente and were designed to make permanent conditions which Hungary and the other states considered unjust. Hungary is in favor of a federation, let it be repeated, but it must be based on the equality of all members.

Autonomy of Transylvania might help on the federation of neighboring states: the larger federation would surely help Transylvania and other territories, Macedonia, for example, which face similar problems.

In advocating federation of neighboring Central European states, the Peasant Parties are speaking for a larger constituency than their own membership. If an honest plebiscite could be held today in the smaller nations of

* Its head offices formerly in Vienna are now in New York.

Eastern Europe and Mid-Europe, an overwhelming majority of the people would vote for federation. Before the monstrous purpose to divide Europe into two zones of influence was launched, every leading statesman of the small nations had declared himself in favor of it. Mr. Sikerski, Polish Prime Minister; Mr. Benes, President of Czechoslovakia; King Peter of Yugoslavia and his Government; the leading political figures of Austria and Hungary; the Slovak leader, Mr. Milan Hodža; the Greek King and his Government; the Bulgarian peasant leader; Mr. Maniu of Roumania, as has been said; all favored federation and in public meetings stated their willingness to accept it, and they made statements to the same effect to leaders in neighboring states.

The plan for a Danubian Federation has received the enthusiastic endorsement of men from these lands now living in other countries. Almost a million American citizens of Magyar origin through their representatives accepted it as the best hope of the future, provided it was based on equal rights for all the member nations, and so stated in convention in 1941; the vote was unanimous. Other racial groups living in America have expressed the same opinion.

All the peoples living in "the European danger zone" under the threat of German or Russian interference, (we remember that it stretches from the Baltic to the Mediterranean), have long looked to organized collaboration as their salvation, always provided it is based on the equality of all member nations and their self determination. Only this policy can secure lasting peace for one hundred million people.

From the hosts of men who want federation we can quote only a few.

Kossuth wanted it. "In heaven's name, I beg Slav and Roumanian brethren," he wrote, "to throw a veil over the past, and to rise, hand in hand for our common freedom." In May 1849, Hungarian, Polish, Bohemian, Roumanian and Serbian delegates were discussing federation. In November 1849 Kossuth was negotiating with the Polish emigrants, and putting forward the project that the small nations must form a United States of Eastern Europe under the protection of Poland, Hungary and Turkey. In June 1850 he explained his plan to Count Laszlo Teleki, referring to the United States as a model organization. He explained it also to the Hungarians in Paris and London, where it was much discussed. He propounded a similar plan to Mazzini in Italy, and through him sent it to other leaders of European reform. All the programs still breathe his passionate hope to unite the small nations of Europe. This last plan, when Kossuth went to London, was published in Cobden's paper, the *Daily News.**

"Danubian Federation was not new to the English political mind," says Stephen Gal† (abbreviated). "While in late '48 Palmerston had declared that the Austrian Monarchy was a European necessity, six months later he held that the monarchy was superanuated and due to collapse without the aid of Russia.

"Kossuth's plan for a confederation underwent changes during his exile, but always he wanted the whole organism

* Exposé de la future organization de la Hongrie.
† Kossuth, America and the Danubian Confederation, by Stephen Gal, historian, The Hungarian Quarterly, Vol. VI.

protected by a great western bulwark. He aimed at no less than a union of all nations and peoples between the Baltic, Adriatic, Black and Mediterranean Seas. The center remained always Hungary, with Poland and Turkey, or Italy and Poland, or sometimes with Turkey alone. This confederation depended on Hungary's independence; if Hungary was freed, Europe would be liberated; if defeated, she would be a martyr to European freedom."

"Half Europe, from Scandinavia through Belgium down to Portugal and the isles of the Mediterranean, was in a fever of excitement, aroused by his personality. Received in England with incredible enthusiasm, Cobden said Kossuth was the greatest man who ever had set foot on English soil. He wrote of him, 'He is certainly a phenomenon; he is not only the first orator of his age, but he unites the qualities of a great administrator with a high morality and an indefatigable courage.'

"The fundamental thesis of Kossuth's lectures in England was, Freedom is the greatest treasure of human life, the warrant of happiness. Constitutional freedom relies on two fortresses, England and America. If the fate of Europe were decided without the intervention of Great Britain, she would cease to be a great power; if despotism were victorious on the continent, Russian Cossacks would water their horses in the Thames and England's freedom would end. 'England and America!' he cried 'do not forget in your proud security those who are oppressed. Save those millions of the people who otherwise would bleed to death.' "*

Kossuth cried his hope to a listening world.

After having in vain demanded Kossuth's extradition, Prince Schwarzenberg had the intention, with the help of

* Ibid., Stephen Gal abbreviated.

the Sublime Porte, to detain him and other Hungarian leaders in Asia Minor for at least five years, until the pacification of Hungary was concluded. But the Sultan released Kossuth to the United States where it was hoped that he would remain for the rest of his life. The United States offered him and his followers a tract of land.

Count Teleki also wanted federation. Dorothy Thompson in 1941 supports the statement of others. "I took from Count Teleki's office a monograph which he had written upon the structure of European nations. A distinguished geographer, he was developing a plan for regional federations, based upon geographic and economic realities." Winston Churchill looks forward to federation. "It is my earnest hope," he says, "that we shall attain the largest common measure of the integrated life of Europe that is possible without destroying the individual characteristics and traditions of its many ancient and historic races. All this I believe will be found to harmonize with the high permanent interests of Britain, the United States, and Russia. It certainly cannot be accomplished without their cordial and concerted agreement and direct participation. Thus and thus only will the glory of Europe rise again."†

At the Moscow Conference, October 1943, Mr. Hull, representing the United States, and Mr. Eden, representing Great Britain, had blue prints of Danubian Federation. But Russia did not want consideration given their plans at the time. They could only be considered, Russia said, by the permanent governments of the states within the Danubian area, not then restored, not by the temporary Governments. On this point Russia may well have been right.

† From the speech of Prime Minister Winston Churchill broadcast, recorded by *The New York Times*, March 22, 1943.

There can be no doubt that plans for Danubian Federation will be introduced at the Peace Conference. It is earnestly to be hoped that Russia will in due time approve.

Timid folk opposed to such a federation point out the antagonism between the Central European peoples. These, we believe, are exaggerated. In the capitols of the great powers the disciples of power politics, some of them in high places, promote them. Certain it is that the small nations are not propagating dissension. They are not the ones who block the road to lasting peace. The alternatives are clear cut, inevitable: federation, or as soon as the wounds of this war are staunched then another.

We cannot forget in these considerations that the chaos existing in unfederated Eastern Europe tempted Germany to economic infiltration, then to dominance and in the end to war. Had the region lying between her and Russia been a confederation of autonomous states, history might have run a different course. It is no unfriendliness toward Russia, nor any ingratitude, to hope that no such temptation will lie at her doors, perhaps almost forcing her in her own way to create unity and inertia, if not peace. Decidedly it is for the good of Russia and Germany that federation in Central Europe be allowed to heal the existing disunity. But why, if federation is so desirable for Central Europe and world peace, has it not come long since? Every time the plan for Danubian Federation becomes practical and immediate, as has been told, one of the great powers stops it. The great power would have to give up something, and so refuses the necessary sanction. For example, a Polish-Czechoslovak and a separate Yugo-Greek pact had been signed by their respective governments. The great powers intervened, and the plans for federation had to be dropped. Quite recently another federation, including Macedonia, Serbia, Yugoslavia, and Bulgaria, was signed and ready to go into effect when one great power stopped it, and the nations lost a promising chance to end the trouble provoking Macedonian problem.

Transylvania presents a situation in relation to Danubian Federation that in the main is identical with that of Macedonia in regard to the Yugoslav federation. In both regions collaboration between the several states would have quenched smouldering fires, for the great advantage of the states involved, and also for the peace of the world. A big power dissented and that chance to further world stability was lost.

While the several great powers may well be urged to take every opportunity for federation into the most careful consideration, and where practical be urged to act, it must be remembered that they carry terrifying responsibilities. As the United Nations become strong in collaboration, let it be said again, the world can but hope they will be able to foster regional federations, looking to the global federation which yonder across the years may come.

Who wants federation? As the French say, "It is to laugh," Listen! Look! The great of the earth have fought for it. There is not a history of Central European peoples that does not approach it. May Transylvania attain autonomy by her federated neighbors.

XX

EVENTS PRECEDING COUNT TELEKI'S DEATH

ON MARCH 27, 1941, by a Palace Revolution in Belgrade, Yugoslavia deposed its collaborationist Regent, Prince Paul, and placed Prince Peter, then eighteen years of age, on the throne. The new King at once renounced the existing treaty of collaboration with Germany.

On April 1st, Mr. Bardossy, Hungarian Minister for Foreign Affairs, was summoned to Vienna to meet the German Minister, Mr. Ribbentrop, who presented him with a German ultimatum, demanding that Hungary allow German troops to cross Hungary in order to attack Yugoslavia, and also demanding that she give whatever war materials and transportation Germany might demand. The ultimatum required instant acceptance, but the Hungarian Minister with difficulty got two days in which to follow proper procedure. He reported to the Prime Minister, Count Teleki.

On April 3, before the two days granted had expired, the Hungarian Government gave an evasive reply, pointing out the advantages of Hungarian neutrality.

At midnight, April 5–6, the German minister to Hungary, Baron Erdmannsdorf, demanded an immediate interview with the Prime Minister, who was working in his study, and received him. He informed Count Teleki that his Government did not believe the Hungarian Government to be in a position to reject Germany's demand because the Chief of the German Staff had already concluded an agreement with the Chief of the Hungarian Staff, General Werth, allowing German troops to cross Hungary, and the German troops were already on their way within Hungary.

After the German Minister had left him Count Teleki wrote a letter to the Regent, Admiral Horthy, instructing his secretary to deliver it at eight o'clock the following morning. The letter was delivered to the Regent, but as it never has been seen since its contents are unknown.

That morning Count Teleki's valet found him dead in his bed: he had committed suicide. He had been left uninformed of the secret General Staff agreement, and had been given no chance to oppose it. His authority as Prime Minister and that of his cabinet had been treacherously ignored. Hungary and Yugoslavia had made a treaty providing against exactly what had happened. Only by suicide could Count Teleki protest his own and his government's innocence to the world and make his protest heard.

On the same day at eleven o'clock German tanks began rolling through Budapest while over the city huge bombers flew low. At four o'clock the helpless Regent appointed Mr. Bardossy Prime Minister, and he immediately began collaboration with Germany. Hungary was plunged into the Second World War on Germany's side.

Already Germany had invaded Austria and Czechoslovakia, encircled Hungary's northern and western borders, and made her position hopeless. Germany was beginning her planned world conquest. Could Hungary have stayed out of the war, could she have remained neutral? Emphatically, we are not discussing these questions. Instead we are stating how she entered the war, and how Count Teleki protested in the only way he could to make the world hear him and understand.

General Werth, Chief of the Hungarian General Staff, was wholly unauthorized to make any agreement with Germany, such authority was outside his duty and command. He acted against his Government's will, and without its knowledge. He was called "traitor" in the Hungarian Parliament. He was an Austrian of German descent.

Although the next events happened two and a half years later they should be mentioned here. On October 15th, 1944, German troops surrounded the residence of the Regent, the Royal Palace, killed the six hundred Palace Guards to the last man, captured the Regent, and took him, his wife, and his two year old grandson to Germany, where after Germany fell he was reported to have been "captured" by the Allies.

A few days after the removal of the Regent, the Holy Crown of St. Stephen, given King Stephen by Pope Sylvester II in the year 1000, was removed from its safe in the Royal Palace by the Germans and carried off to Germany, where suggestively it was said to have been deposited with the German Crown Jewels. Later reports have stated that it had been discovered by the Allies.

And Count Teleki, himself a Transylvanian, before the upheaval had been working on the scientific basis for Danubian federation. He was a distinguished statesman, a noted scholar, and one of the greatest of world geographers. His basic conviction is quoted at the beginning of this book, "Europe is a unit creating its own form of life which in the course of its development cannot but become a single community." Regional unities, fundamentally geographic, perhaps expressing themselves first politically in autonomy, would be led through recognition of their mutual concerns toward federation. So ultimately Europe will become one great community. Every regional unity is therefore tremendously important. Such is the background for his minute presentation of Transylvanian regional unity. Despite its diversity, it is truly one and should be indivisible, and it has attained a regional consciousness. Economically all parts of it, with different altitudes, soil and climate, predestine its inhabitants to certain advantages, and these are supplementary, not antagonistic; regional consciousness grows from them.

Count Teleki's statement about Transylvanian unity is the result of life long consideration, the product of endless effort, it gives the scientific facts, it is authoritative. Every reader should study it carefully. It will be found in Appendix 5.

XXI

AGAIN THE THIRD
ALTERNATIVE

COUNT PAUL TELEKI, Prime Minister of Hungary, wrote
a memorable study of Transylvania. He killed himself
when the Germans without permission started crossing
Hungary to attack Yugoslavia. This was his protest. After
the Big Powers had failed for a year to make peace practical, many people all over the world were profoundly discouraged. They had believed that progress would be made
toward coordination, they had been sharing Mr. Churchill's
hope. At Paris it became apparent that what the Transylvanians wanted, or any other people destined to readjust-
ment of boundaries and governments, had little part in
shaping what they got. Why discuss what they want and
what they ought to have? Mr. Churchill speaks of "the
iron curtain" that divides Western from Eastern Europe,
and the world fears it.

The Powers have decided to give all Transylvania back
to Roumania, including that northern part which Roumania at Germany's command returned to Hungary. The
United States alone protested. The plea of Hungary for
reconsideration of the whole matter, a document prepared
with meticulous care, was not even heard. It was agreed,

however, that the matter could be reopened when the twenty-one nations met in conference. Whether this gesture will have the force of world opinion behind it remains to be seen. Meanwhile why discuss what the Transylvanians want, and what they ought to have?

But surely what a people located in a certain territory want ought to be considered. Government, "of the people, by the people, and for the people" demands it. Their aspirations grow out of the very soil and their reasoned conclusions will last for long, probably until in one way or another down the years the Government of Transylvania expresses the will of her people, the three peoples, or "nations," of Transylvania, the old Roumanian settlers, the Saxons, and the Magyars. They all want some form of autonomous self government. They are far nearer agreement in this common purpose than is usually known or admitted. This alone is reason enough for looking the facts in the face.

The old Transylvanian Roumanians, long resident in the territory, have given proof of what they want. They resent the incredible practices usually associated with the Orient in their Transylvanian homeland where before they were unknown.* These men want autonomy.

They gave good evidence of it after the First World War. Their leaders in 1918 held a meeting at Gyulafehervar, and passed significant resolutions. We quote those best witnessing the essential togetherness of the leaders of the three peoples, and expressing the regional consciousness already mentioned.†

Resolution "III. 1. Complete national (racial) liberty for all peoples living together. Each people shall have the

* See Panariote system, Chapter XIV.
† See Chapter XIX.

right to be educated and governed in its own language by its own administration through its own elected representatives. In the legislative assemblies and in the Government of the country each people shall have a share proportionate to its number.

"2. All religious beliefs shall have equal rights and full religious autonomy shall prevail.

"3. True democracy to be established in all domains of the public life. Proportional representation on general, direct, equal, and secret ballot for both sexes over twenty-one years of age in communal, municipal, and legislative elections.

"4. Full freedom of press and right of assembly; free propagation of human thought."*

Such was the plan of the Roumanians of Transylvania at the end of the First World War; but it was not in the least the intention of the Roumanian Government in Bucharest, which had plans wholly different.

None the less there has been constant agitation for autonomy down to the present time. In the early twenties the Peasant Party (Taranist), their strongest political group, put a plank in their platform that Transylvania must become autonomous within Greater Roumania. And throughout these succeeding years this policy has been constantly advocated by Julius Maniu, himself a Transylvanian Roumanian, who throughout a long public career has proved himself a truly democratic leader and Roumanian patriot. A man of marked ability he never has surrendered to the corruption around him, and he fought Nazism in Roumania at his personal peril. It is to be observed that such Transylvanian autonomy as these and

* Andrew Rónai, translated from "Transylvania," Budapest, 1940.

other Roumanians in Transylvania have advocated, might later prove to be a step toward Danubian Federation, and to Transylvanian autonomy within it.

The second Transylvanian group, the Saxons, have long favored an autonomous Transylvania, and for the same reason that the established Transylvanian Roumanians have wanted it. If given the chance, they no doubt would loyally support autonomy under Greater Roumania. The alleged removal of seventy thousand of them to Russia, perhaps a larger number, is screened by what Mr. Churchill calls "the iron curtain." We have said that such deportations of populations are the utmost infringement of human rights, the very last barbarity. But here we are discussing the attitude of Transylvanian Saxons to the autonomy of Transylvania. Can it be doubted that they would prefer autonomy, their rights preserved through centuries of Magyar rule, to what they apparently are getting?

The third group, the Magyars, residents in Transylvania for a thousand years since the leadership of Arpad, would welcome any stable return to rule and order. This book is a part of their testimony, there is no need of repetition.

Here then is the recent decision by the powers, May 1946, excepting the United States, to turn Transylvanian rule back to Roumania, with the rather feeble assurance that it may later be reviewed by the Conference. For the sake of the discussion, let it be agreed that Transylvania wants autonomy. This is important, but what reasons have we to hope that this decision for Roumanian rule made lately will ever be reconsidered?

It is to be remembered that such reconsideration is nothing less than the order of the day. Hungary has become a republic, the King of Italy has departed to involuntary exile, it is said in Portugal other monarchs appear to be on the march, the very foundations of European governments are changing. Russia's "Iron curtain," as Mr. Churchill calls it, is likely to swing to and fro. Fifty-one nations* are soon assembling to begin their endless task of coordinating human life on this planet. If anything is predictable it is that momentary fixities, however impressive, will change. Only a few years back Russia herself began a new regime.

Observe another great change. International mindedness in the United States was lacking in wide sections at the time of the First World War. Today it is dominant. The radio, the bombs, all the flashing changes that have brought us to the consciousness of Mr. Willkie's "One World," have meaning for Transylvania. We need infinite patience. We need something else; a determination to keep telling the truth about Transylvania, this mighty, glorious, and distressed area, until at last the consulting nations shall **agree** on justice, and give Transylvania autonomy, and this may be within the framework of the United Nations itself. The day will come! The French still sing, "Ca ira! Ca ira! Ca ira."

The issue depends on the intelligent will of the world, what you and I believe and millions like us, plain folk the world over. Kossuth took for his slogan the answer of the man who swam a long distance out to his ship. "How could you do it?" asked Kossuth. The man answered, "Where there is the will nothing is impossible." When enough people think straight about autonomy for Transylvania it will come. Nothing is impossible where there is the will!

* More nations are applying for United Nation Membership.

And as we hope and work for it, it is well for us to remember that we are not alone. On a clear night look up at the starlit sky and see stretching across it the broad misty belt of the Milky Way. Once Hungarians believed that its stars were the sparks struck off by the silver shoes on the horses hoofs as the mighty warriors of the past rode to rescue hard-pressed Magyars wherever they might be. The great of the past ride today with the great of the present to bring lasting peace to the nations, and we shall yet establish it! Transylvania will come into her own. Let the Milky Way still be to us the promise set in the heavens that the hosts ride with us.

Appendix

Contents.

Appendix 1

THE MOSCOW-ROUMANIAN ARMISTICE

U. S. DEPARTMENT OF STATE

SEPTEMBER 13, 1944
No. 431

The following are the terms of the Roumanian armistice agreement which has been signed in Moscow:

"AGREEMENT BETWEEN THE GOVERNMENTS OF THE UNITED STATES OF AMERICA, THE SOVIET UNION, AND THE UNITED KINGDOM ON THE ONE HAND, AND THE GOVERNMENT OF ROUMANIA ON THE OTHER CONCERNING AN ARMISTICE.

"The Government and High Command of Roumania, recognizing the fact of the defeat of Roumania in the war against the Union of Soviet Socialist Republics, the United States of America, and the United Kingdom, and the other United Nations, accept the armistice terms presented by the Governments of the above mentioned three Allied Powers, acting in the interests of all the United Nations.

"On the basis of the foregoing the representative of the Allied (Soviet) High Command, Marshal of the Soviet Union, R. Y. Malinovski, duly authorized thereto by the Governments of the United States of America, the Soviet Union, and the

United Kingdom, acting in the interests of all the United Nations, on the one hand, and the representatives of the Government and High Command of Roumania, Minister of State and Minister of Justice L. Patrascanu, Deputy Minister of Internal Affairs, Adjutant of His Majesty the King of Roumania, General D. Damaceanu, Prince Stirbey, and Mr. G. Popp, on the other hand holding full powers, have signed the following conditions:

"1. As from August 24, 1944, at four a.m., Roumania has entirely discontinued military operations against the Union of Soviet Socialist Republics on all theatres of war, has withdrawn from the war against the United Nations, has broken off relations with Germany and her satellites, has entered the war and will wage war on the side of the Allied Powers against Germany and Hungary for the purpose of restoring Roumanian independence and sovereignty, for which purpose she provides not less than twelve divisions with corps troops.

"Military operations on the part of Roumanian armed forces, including naval and air forces, against Germany and Hungary will be conducted under the general leadership of the Allied (Soviet) High Command.

"2. The Government and High Command of Roumania undertake to take steps for the disarming and interning of the armed forces of Germany and Hungary on Roumanian territory *and also for the interning of the citizens of both states mentioned who reside there.* (See Annex to Article Two)*

"3. The Government and High Command of Roumania will ensure to the Soviet and other Allied forces facilities for free movement on Roumanian territory in any direction if required by the military situation, the Roumanian Government and High Command of Roumania giving such movement every possible assistance with their own means of communications and at their own expense on land, on water and in the air. (See Annex to Article Three)

* Italics the author's.

"4. The state frontier between the Union of Soviet Socialist Republics and Roumania, established by the Soviet-Roumanian Agreement of June 8, 1940, is restored.

"5. The Government and High Command of Roumania will immediately hand over all Soviet and Allied prisoners of war in their hands, as well as interned citizens and citizens forcibly removed to Roumania, to the Allied (Soviet) High Command for the return of these persons to their own country.

"From the moment of the signing of the present terms and until repatriation the Roumanian Government and High Command undertake to provide at their own expense all Soviet and Allied prisoners of war, as well as forcibly removed and interned citizens, and displaced persons and refugees, with adequate food, clothing and medical service, in accordance with hygienic requirements, as well as with means of transport for the return of all those persons to their own country.

"6. The Roumanian Government will immediately set free, irrespective of citizenship and nationality, all persons held in confinement on account of their activities in favor of the United Nations or because of their sympathies with the cause of the United Nations, or because of their racial origin, and will repeal all discriminatory legislation and restrictions imposed thereunder.

"7. The Roumanian Government and High Command undertake to hand over as trophies into the hands of the Allied (Soviet) High Command all war material of Germany and her satellites located on Roumanian territory, including vessels of the fleet of Germany and her satellites located in Roumanian waters.

"8. The Roumanian Government and High Command undertake not to permit the export or expropriation of any form of property (including valuables and currency) belonging to Germany, Hungary or to their nationals or to persons resident in their territories or in territories occupied by them without the permission of the Allied (Soviet) High Command. They will keep this property in such manner as may be prescribed by the Allied (Soviet) High Command.

"9. The Roumanian Government and High Command under- take to hand over to the Allied (Soviet) High Command all vessels belonging or having belonged to the United Nations which are located in Roumanian ports, no matter at whose dis- posal these vessels may be, for the use of the Allied (Soviet) High Command during the period of the war against Germany and Hungary in the general interests of the Allies, these vessels subsequently to be returned to their owners.

"The Roumanian Government bear the full material responsi- bility for any damage or destruction of the aforementioned property until the moment of the transfer of this property to the Allied (Soviet) High Command.

"10. The Roumanian Government must make regular pay- ments in Roumanian currency required by the Allied (Soviet) High Command for the fulfillment of its functions and will in case of need ensure the use on Roumanian territory of industrial and transportation enterprises, means of communication, power stations, enterprises and installations of public utility, stores of fuel, fuel oil, food and other materials, and services in accord- ance with instructions issued by the Allied (Soviet) High Com- mand.

"Roumanian merchant vessels, whether in Roumanian or for- eign waters, shall be subject to the operational control of the Allied (Soviet) High Command for use in the general interest of the Allies. (See Annex to Article Ten)

"11. Losses caused to the Soviet Union by military opera- tions and by the occupation by Roumania of Soviet territory will be made good by Roumania to the Soviet Union, but, taking into consideration that Roumania has not only withdrawn from the war, but has declared war and in fact is waging war against Germany and Hungary, the parties agree that compensation for the indicated losses will be made by Roumania not in full but only in part, namely to the amount of three hundred million United States dollars payable over six years in commodities (oil products, grain, timber products, seagoing and river craft, sundry machinery, et cetera).

"Compensation will be paid by Roumania for losses caused to the property of other Allied states and their nationals in Roumania during the war, the amount of compensation to be fixed at a later date. (See Annex to Article Eleven)

"12. The Roumanian Government undertakes within the periods indicated by the Allied (Soviet) High Command to return to the Soviet Union in complete good order all valuables and materials removed from its territory during the war, belonging to state, public and cooperative organizations, enterprises, institutions or individual citizens, such as: factory and works equipment, locomotives, railway trucks, tractors, motor vehicles, historic monuments, museum valuables and any other property.

"13. The Roumanian Government undertakes to restore all legal rights and interests of the United Nations and their nationals on Roumanian territory as they existed before the war and to return their property in complete good order.

"14. The Roumanian Government and High Command undertake to collaborate with the Allied (Soviet) High Command in the apprehension and trial of persons accused of war crimes.

"15. The Roumanian Government undertakes immediately to dissolve all pro-Hitler organizations (of a Fascist type) situated in Roumanian territory, whether political, military or paramilitary, as well as other organizations conducting propaganda hostile to the United Nations, in particular to the Soviet Union, and will not in future permit the existence of organizations of that nature.

"16. The printing, importation and distribution in Roumania of periodical and non-periodical literature, the presentation of theatrical performances and films, the work of wireless stations, post, telegraph and telephone shall be carried out in agreement with the Allied (Soviet) High Command. (See Annex to Article Sixteen)

"17. Roumanian Civil Administration is restored in the whole area of Roumania separated by not less than fifty-one hundred kilometres (depending upon conditions of terrain) from the front line, Roumanian administrative bodies undertaking to carry out, in the interests of the reestablishment of peace and security, instructions and orders of the Allied (Soviet) High Command issued by them for the purpose of securing the execution of these armistice terms.

"18. An Allied Control Commission will be established which will undertake until the conclusion of peace the regulation of and control over the execution of the present terms under the general direction and orders of the Allied (Soviet) High Command, acting on behalf of the Allied Powers. (See Annex to Article Eighteen)

"19. The Allied Governments regard the decision of the Vienna award regarding Transylvania as null and void and are agreed that Transylvania (or the greater part thereof) should be returned to Roumania, subject to confirmation at the peace settlement, and the Soviet Government agrees that Soviet forces shall take part for this purpose in joint military operations with Roumania against Germany and Hungary.

"20. The present terms come into force at the moment of their signing.

"Done in Moscow, in four copies, each in the Russian, English and Roumanian languages, the Russian and English texts being authentic. September 12, 1944.

"*By authority of the Governments of the United States of America,** the Union of Soviet Socialist Republics and the United Kingdom.

"By authority of the Government and High Command of Roumania.

"Annex to the Armistice Agreement between the Govern-

* Italics the author's.

ments of the United States of America, the Soviet Union, and the United Kingdom on the one hand and the Government of Roumania on the other hand.

"A. Annex to Article 2.

"The measures provided for in Article 2 of the agreement regarding the internment of citizens of Germany and Hungary now in Roumanian territory do not extend to citizens of those countries of Jewish origin.

"B. Annex to Article 3.

"Under cooperation of the Roumanian Government and High Command of Roumania, mentioned in Article 3 of the Agreement, is understood the placing at the disposal of the Allied (Soviet) High Command for use at its discretion during the armistice all Roumanian military, air and naval constructions and installations, ports, harbors, barracks, warehouses, airfields, means of communication, meteorological stations which might be required for military needs in complete good order and with the personnel required for their maintenance.

"C. Annex to Article 10.

"The Roumanian Government will withdraw and redeem within such time limits and on such terms as the Allied (Soviet) High Command may specify, all holdings in Roumanian territory of currencies issued by the Allied (Soviet) High Command, and will hand over currency so withdrawn free of cost to the Allied (Soviet) High Command.

"D. Annex to Article 11.

"The basis for settlements of payment of compensation provided for in Article 11 of the present Agreement will be the American dollar at its gold parity on the day of signing of the Agreement, i.e. thirty-five dollars for one ounce of gold.

"E. Annex to Article 16.

"The Roumanian Government undertakes that wireless communication, telegraphic and postal correspondence, correspondence in cypher and courier correspondence, as well as telephonic communication with foreign countries of Embassies,

Legations and Consulates situated in Roumania, will be conducted in the manner laid down by the Allied (Soviet) High Command.

"F. Annex to Article 18.

"Control over the exact execution of the armistice terms is entrusted to the Allied Control Commission to be established in conformity with Article 18 of the Armistice Agreement.

"The Roumanian Government and their organs shall fulfill all instructions of the Allied Control Commission arising out of the Armistice Agreement.

"The Allied Control Commission will set up special organs or sections entrusting them respectively with the execution of various functions. In addition, the Allied Control Commission may have its officers in various parts of Roumania.

"The Allied Control Commission will have its seat in the City of Bucharest.

"Moscow: September 12, 1944."

Appendix 2

BRITISH-FRENCH DRAFT OF UNION

The following proposal for collaboration between England and France was presented to the French Government by the British Ambassador on June 16, 1940. The draft Declaration of Union proposing the merging of the British and French Empires reads as follows:

"At this most fateful moment in the history of the modern world, the Government of the United Kingdom and the French Republic make this declaration of indissoluble union and unyielding resolution in their common defense of justice and freedom against subjection to a system which reduces mankind to a life of robots and slaves.

"The two governments declare that France and Great Britain shall no longer be two, but one Franco-British Union. The Constitution of the Union will provide for joint organs of defense, foreign, financial, and economic policies. Every citizen of France will enjoy immediately citizenship of Great Britain. Every British subject will become a citizen of France.

"Both countries will share responsibility for the repair of the devastation of war where it occurs in their territories, and the resources of both shall be equally and as one applied to that purpose.

"During the war there shall be a single War Cabinet and all the forces of Britain and France, whether on land, sea, or in the air, will be placed under its direction. It will govern from wherever it best can. The two parliaments will be formally associated.

"The nations of the British Empire are already forming new armies. France will keep her available forces in the field, on the sea, and in the air.

"The Union appeals to the United States to fortify the economic resources of the Allies and to bring her powerful material aid to the common cause. The Union will concentrate its whole energy against the power of the enemy, no matter where the battle may be, and thus we shall conquer."*

* Supplied by British Information Services, New York, N. Y. Owing to the war France never replied.

Appendix 3

SAXONS

BY JOSEPH DEER AND BELA PUKANSZKY

Reprinted by permission from Erdely (Budapest, 1940) and here first
pubished in English.

Saxon research has produced many valuable works on
the history of the Transylvania Saxons. It has paid special
attention to the question of origin. On the basis of a linguistic comparison of dialects, the regions on the left bank
of the Rhine, the Moselle districts and Luxemburg, long
were believed to be the original home of the Saxons. New
researches, however, conclude that there was no single region of origin. In view of their conglomerate character, the
Saxons do not differ from any other large group of settlers.
A great majority of them undoubtedly came from the
Rhine and Moselle regions. The dialects spoken in the
latter places resemble most closely that of the Saxons.

The first authentic records generally refer to the Saxons
as "Flandrenses" or simply "Teutonici." The name "Saxons," in general usage today, first appeared in the early
13th century, and thereafter gradually replaced the word
"Teutonici" altogether.

The bulk of the Saxon immigration into Transylvania,
it has been definitely established, occurred in the middle

of the 12th century. They entered the country on the invitation of King Géza II (1141–1161). Approximately 200 villages were settled as the result of this colonization.

The settling of the Saxons in Transylvania, however, was only a chapter in the large-scale German migration to the east in the Middle Ages. Like other German settlers in countries neighboring on Hungary, the Saxons brought with them their settlement law, their village type, and their economic order. They were free farmers, led into their new country by so-called "locators," managers of colonization. The latter gradually developed into a leading class. The mode of life of the Saxons was transplanted into their new homeland without any particular difficulty. They paid land rent, performed military duties, and elected their own village magistrates and priests freely. This primitive autonomy, moving within the scope of the village, was independent of the policies of the recipient state. It was a basic condition of settlement included in and dependent upon the agreement between the "locator" and the landlord.

Much depended, therefore, on the landlord. If he was only the proprietor of a private estate in need of farmers, the settlement remained simply a private enterprise. If, however, the landlord was the king himself, the settlement became a problem of general, economic, political and military concern. In the latter case, the newcomers came into direct contact with the administration, enjoyed its protection and were able to maintain their separate existence as an ethnic entity. Good examples of the first private estate type, were to be found in the German colonization in Poland, and a typical example of the second sort, where the king himself was the landlord, was furnished by the settlement of the Saxons in Transylvania.

The Saxon "guests" were considered a "people of the King," and the land on which they settled was crown property. From the beginning they were under government supervision and protection. They possessed not only village autonomies, common in East Central Europe, but a special organization established by the central government. This method assured the Saxons an autonomous life untouched by the various administrative branches of the country. There were several larger Saxon settlement areas: the Királyföld ("King's Land") around Nagyszeben, the Barcaság (Burzenland) and the Beszterce area. Originally the settlers of the Nagyszeben area were organized in counties (*comitatus*), set up by the administration, with royal officials heading them. The latter collected taxes, led the militia, and administered higher justice.

The Kings of Hungary considered not only the hardly inhabited mountainous peripheries of the Carpathian Basin as their own, but also those ethnic elements which were appointed for the cultivation and defense of these areas. The legal status of these "peoples of the King" was one of the determining factors in the development of the Transylvania Saxons.

According to the plans of the Arpad Kings, any people adjudged able to take part in the colonization, cultivation and defense of the border regions, was, for that very purpose, given this privileged status. In Transylvania not only the Saxons were "people of the King" but also, for instance, the Székelys. Thus, when the wave of German peasant settlers reached Hungary in the 12th century, they found there a well-organized state, able to utilize their agricultural and fighting abilities, and to define their rights and obligations. The German historian Hermann Aubin has explained the nature of Hungarian-German relations in the Middle Ages, as compared with the relations between the German settlers and the Slavic peoples, by stating that in the case of Hungary "Germany found itself faced by a state which consolidated very early, had its independent church organization, and possessed a geographically compact territory."

As in Poland, the influence of European feudalism made itself felt in Hungary by the 13th century. The upper strata of the nobility, acquiring large estates, began to take over the leading rôles in political life. It could not endanger, however, the unity of the state. This condition was due partly to the fact that Hungarian Kings found methods to counteract feudalism. Hungary did not become a "republic of the nobility." From the early 13th century, the kings tried to organize different social groups against the feudal lords, creating veritable strongholds for the former (*universitas, communitas*) with constitutional support. By the end of the Middle Ages these were granted autonomy on more or less wide scale. Such autonomous bodies were the counties (*comitatus*) themselves. These were first royal administrative districts, later to become autonomous bodies governed by the local nobility. These corresponded, in the border areas, to autonomies of ethnic groups. First among the latter were the Transylvanian Saxons, enabled through the *Andreanum,* a charter issued by the King Andrew II in 1224, to tread the path leading to full autonomy.

The Andreanum dissolved the system of the old Saxon counties, integrating all Saxons of the Nagyszeben area into one people (*"unua sit populus"*), placing at their head a high royal official, the *Comes* of Szeben, usually one of the high dignitaries of the country. To prevent the *Comes*

(Count) from transforming his official position into that
of the feudal landlord of the Saxons—a phenomenon not
uncommon in European feudalism—the old royal counties
received autonomy, their inhabitants electing their judges
among themselves. The *Comes* was not supposed to send his
own agents, *officiales*, among the Saxons. These old counties became the foundations of the later Saxon "seats"
(*sedes*, districts). The number of the latter was originally
three, rising to seven in the 14th century. They were headed
by Saxon district judges. This co-operation of central and
local administration in the Saxon area corresponded to the
roles of the *comites*, representing the King, on the one hand,
and of the judges elected by the nobility on the other, in
the autonomous Hungarian counties.

The unity assured by the *Andreanum* was not only legal
and administrative but territorial as well. Originally, the
Saxon settlements in the Szeben area did not constitute a
compact unit, many other, Székely, Petcheneg and Roumanian colonies being wedged between them. The King
transplanted the latter into other districts, promising the
Saxons that no high dignitary was to receive any grants of
properties on Saxon territory. This enabled the Saxons to
maintain a certain uniform character in the social and
economic field within their autonomy, to preserve their
tongue and nationality, and to survive through long centuries in compact ethnic units even to our own day.

In mediaeval Hungary, there was no single serious attempt to suppress the liberties of the Saxons. The Golden
Bull (*Bulla Aurea*), issued in 1222, and considered by
many historians as the "Hungarian Magna Carta," stated
explicitly that the King should "guard the rights originally
granted to the guests, irrespective of their nationality."

The legal struggle for prerogatives thus created a natural connection between the Saxons and the Hungarian Estates, which solidarity led to a "union," an alliance, between the Hungarian nobility, the Székelys and the Saxons of Transylvania as early as the beginning of the 15th century.

Though King Charles Robert, restorer of the royal power, found himself opposed by an unsuccessful Saxon revolt in 1317, he did not suppress the liberties of the Saxons. His reform, put into effect in the third decade of the 14th century, was based on the guiding principle of his domestic policy, a proper balance between central administration and local autonomy. The system established by the *Andreanum* could no longer suffice, because a single royal representative, the Count of Szeben, was not able to satisfy the judicial demands of all the Saxon districts. The counties in Transylvania and in all Hungary were governed each by its *Comes,* co-operating with the elected judges. Following this example, so-called "King's judges" were appointed at the head of each Saxon "Seat." They were mostly men of Saxon descent. In consequence, the judicial authority of the Count of Szeben became more or less nominal.

Under the protection of their privileges, the Saxon settlements continued to flourish. During the 14th and 15th centuries, Nagyszeben, Brassó, Segesvár, Beszterce, Szászváros and Szászsebes grew into cities. The period saw the appearance of fortified cities and church-fortresses, which served for religious services and at the same time for protection against potential enemies. Commerce and industry gradually developed. In 1376, when Goblinus, Saxon-born bishop of Transylvania, sent as special envoy of King Louis the Great, attended the meeting of the privileged

Saxon settlements, he found 19 guilds and 25 trades active in the Szeben area.

Political development in Hungary in the 14th century was especially favorable to the completion of autonomy. The social development leading to the formation of Estates was paralleled with the efforts of the privileged to enhance their influence through the joining of other elements of similar legal status. Thus the tendency towards a rapprochement between the four Saxon settlement areas in Transylvania, (the seven "Seats" of the Szeben area, the two Seats of Medgyes and Selyk and, finally, the Barcaság and Beszterce districts) gradually strengthened. This prepared the way for a complete union.

Center and model of Saxon life was the Szeben area which preceded in development the three other areas and exercised a natural attraction on them. While the Szeben area was organized according to the reforms of Charles Robert the other areas were governed on the pattern of the previous administration in Szeben. The Barcaság and Beszterce districts had at their helm the same royal representative, usually the *comes* of the Székelys. These two districts, however, transferred their judicial appeals to the seven Seats of Szeben.

It was King Matthias Corvinus who finally granted full autonomy to the Saxons, thus assuring their unimpaired social and ethnic unity. Matthias desired a strong royal power and endeavored, as far as possible, to curb the influence of the feudal lords. He served this aim not only through reforms in taxation and the military system but also through strengthening those social factors which could be used to support his endeavors.

With successive measures issued after 1464, Matthias

abolished the system of appointed judges, and permitted both the city of Brassó and the Beszterce district to elect their own supreme judges. Yet there remained obstacles of a different nature in the way of full autonomy, obstacles resulting from the social development of the Saxons themselves. The leading class of the Saxons consisted mostly of descendants of the "locators," known as *gräfs* in their own tongue, or in Magyar. The way of living of the Hungarian nobility exercised a profound influence on this Saxon elite. By the end of the 13th century a part of these *gräfs* acted already as if they were nobles (more nobilium se gerentes). They took part in the Diet, and fought in the entourage of the King. Many of them actually acquired nobility, and some were elevated even to the peerage.

This stratum of the Saxons was inclined to acquire privileges for itself and to attempt to perpetuate its official position as hereditary lords of the common Saxons. Many of the "King's judges" appointed during the 14th century were scions of such Saxon families, against whom the people often filed complaints. King Matthias solved this problem in 1469 by authorizing the Seven Seats to expel their judges and to elect new ones according to their free will.

The legal status of the Transylvania Saxons as an autonomous community (Universitas Saxonum Transylvaniae), uniting both in administration and jurisdiction all four Saxon areas, was finally consolidated at the end of the 15th century. Heading the *universitas* was a "King's judge" in the person of the mayor of Nagyszeben. The Saxons won representation in the Diet as a political body, held meetings, like the Croatian Estates, passing statutes of local authority. This made possible the historic role of the Saxons as one of the Transylvania's three "nations."

Protestantism exerted a decisive influence on Saxon mentality. The Saxon *universitas* as a whole accepted the Lutheran faith. Thus an independent church was founded, which became a cohesive force promoting political, linguistic and moral unity. Saxon literature points out how their church is highly valued by the people as an instrument of unification. Besides religious life it has embodied many other manifestations of cultural development. This church, the "Siebenburgisch-sächsische Landeskirche," became one of the strongest supporters of autonomous Saxon development. It outlived the era of royal privileges, the World War and Transylvania's incorporation into Greater Roumania, and remained in the post-war period the only visible organization of Saxon unity.

There were always, however, strong motives making the close co-operation of the Saxon with the other two Transylvania "nations" necessary and desirable. In earlier days, in 1437, common interests and the growing Turkish peril had brought about a defensive alliance of the three "nations." From this date on they met in common Diets. The alliance was renewed several times and proved most effective and even indispensable in the period of Turkish wars and during Transylvanian independence as a separate principality.

Heated debates between the representatives of the three "nations" often occurred in the Diets, especially with regard to the apportionment of the taxes. But their common interests always compelled them to conclude that the perils confronting them could be averted only by their united action.

After the expulsion of the Turks from Hungary, when Transylvania came under the rule of the Hapsburg Kings a number of Saxons thought an opportunity had arrived to place the Saxons under the special protection of the dynasty, which was also of German origin. Viennese statesmen indeed regarded the Saxons as racial brothers and employed every device to insure their political prominence. This dynastic protection would have been enhanced by the dissolution or reorganization of the alliance of the three "nations," the numerically declining Saxons would have been strengthened by the colonization of new German settlers, placed in areas under direct control of the Vienna Military Council.

The majority of the Saxons, however, greeted imperial rule with anything but enthusiasm. Subsequent developments entirely justified their cautious attitude toward the Vienna administration. Vienna's aim was, primarily, to establish absolutist rule. This aim by its very nature was opposed to the traditional system of privileges enjoyed by the Saxons. The religious problem also raised an insurmountable obstacle in the way of co-operation between the Roman Catholic dynasty and the Protestant Saxons. The old alliance between the three Transylvania "nations" was consequently continued.

Baron Samuel Bruckenthal, great Saxon statesman and intellectual pioneer of 18th century enlightenment, was the only person who succeeded in turning the interests of the Vienna government to the advantage of the Saxons. An influential adviser of Maria Theresa after 1753, throughout his public career he remained the faithful son of his people. The higher he went, the more effectively he used his influence on their behalf. He also achieved merit in the field of Saxon cultural advancement. The museum which he founded and which bears his name, together with the Archives of Nagyszeben, represent the most important learned institutions of the Saxons in Transylvania.

The traditional alliance of the three Transylvania "nations" proved most effective in opposing Emperor Joseph II's policy of forced centralization. The Emperor dissolved the Saxon *universitas* as an autonomous body, as he had dissolved other political bodies in Transylvania, seized its wealth, and incorporated the different Seats into the ten counties of Transylvania. Sticking to their traditions, the Saxons stoutly resented the political experiment of Joseph II. Although they fought side by side with the Hungarians and the Székelys for the old constitution of Transylvania, the Emperor decided to introduce German as the official language in his Empire, including Hungary. When on his death bed, Joseph II revoked his unsuccessful reform in 1790, the joy which followed this exceeded even the mourning over the Emperor's death. As the Saxon historian Frederick Teutsch wrote: "A boundless enthusiasm possessed their souls. Nobles and officials, Magyars and Saxons, dined, drank and danced together on the streets in broad daylight."

The 19th century antiquating feudal institutions brought Liberalism and nationalism. The Saxons were confronted with new vital problems, since their *universitas,* as an autonomous body, was also an institution based on feudal traditions. And further, the influence of nationalistic ideas created a new situation so far as concerned the coordination of the different ethnic groups living side by side in Transylvania. The love of a common Transylvania homeland and the idea of traditional co-operation lived in the greater part of the Saxon people. This feeling is expressed in their 19th century national song, the last verse of which runs as follows:

> Siebenbürgen süsse Heimat,
> Unser teures Vaterland,
> Sei gegrüsst in deiner Schöne
> Und um alle deine Söhne
> Schlinge sich der Eintracht Band!

> Transylvania, our sweet country,
> Our dear fatherland,
> Be thou saluted in thy beauty
> And about all thy sons
> May the bond of unity be twined!

This song, an expression of Saxon national consciousness, echoed their desire for the welfare and harmony of all the sons of Transylvania. It symbolizes the willingness with which the Saxons have participated in the common life of the peoples of Transylvania.

Appendix 4

"ROUMANIAN TREATMENT OF HUNGARIAN MINORITIES"

A speech to the League of Nations on Roumanian Treatment of Hungarian Minorities at the Sixth Meeting of the League—September 1934—delivered by the Hon. Tibor Eckhardt, Ph. D., long member of the Hungarian Parliament and Hungarian representative to the League.

PROTECTION OF MINORITIES

General Discussion

M. Eckhardt (Hungary)—The discussion of that part of the report on the work of League of Nations which deals with the question of minorities has, at Hungary's request, been referred to the Sixth Committee. I, therefore, consider it my duty to state the reasons for my government's request.

The question whether the Assembly is competent in the matter of minorities has often been raised in this Committee. This competence is clearly defined in the Covenant, Article 3 of which says:

"The Assembly may deal at its meetings with any matter within the sphere of action of the League or affecting the peace of the world."

The protection of minorities not only comes within the sphere of action of the League of Nations, but undoubtedly takes an important place therein, particularly as the maintenance of peace, and hence the future of Europe, largely depends on the satisfactory position of the European minorities. The Assembly's right to make a careful study of the problem of minorities is, therefore, doubly confirmed by Article 3 of the Covenant.

But this right conferred on the League of Nations is also a duty. As guarantor of the Minorities Treaties concluded after the war, which placed these minorities under its protection, the League of Nations adopted, in 1920, the report of a distinguished statesman, the late M. Tittoni, which clearly defines the exact meaning of the term "guarantee of the League of Nations." According to this report, the League must satisfy itself that the provisions regarding the protection of minorities are constantly applied. The function which the Council has assumed in the course of years in the matter of minorities has been to examine and judge on a legal basis cases of concrete complaints. But it is evident that the League's activities in the sphere of minorities cannot be confined to the work of detail done by the Council, however valuable that may be, and that, as was stated before the Council in 1929, "it is necessary to take steps to enable the League of Nations to keep itself informed of the general evolution of the problem of minorities, to observe and follow this problem closely, and thus to satisfy itself of the fate of the minorities. Only in this way can a true guarantee by the League of Nations be realized and only in this way can the concrete cases brought before it be judged at their true value." It is, therefore, necessary for the Assembly to examine the general position as regards the protection of minorities, to study the efficacy of this protection, to decide what course should be followed and to remove the difficulties which stand in the way of its satisfactory application. Such are the considerations which underlie the Hungarian proposal. In submitting to you this proposal, we also desire to ensure the continuity of a tradition for which credit originally belongs to the Union of South Africa and to Latvia.

While every country has a general right to draw the League's attention to the effective protection of minorities, for Hungary this is a special right conferred on her by the fact that over 30 per cent of the Hungarian people, separated by the Treaty of Trianon from the country that for centuries has been their fatherland, were reduced fifteen years ago to the situation of a minority under foreign rule. In fact, under Articles 44 and 47 of the Treaty of Trianon, the Successor States recognized and confirmed "in relation to Hungary their obligation to accept the embodiment in a treaty with the Principal Allied and Associated Powers such provisions as may be deemed necessary by those Powers to protect the interests of inhabitants of the Successor States who differ from the majority of the population in race, language or religion." This stipulation of the Treaty of Trianon formally gives Hungary a right of supervision over the lot of the Hungarian minorities in the Successor States.

Moreover, when Hungary was called upon to sign the Treaty of Trianon, she only brought herself to do so in consideration of the formal and solemn promise contained in the covering letter annexed to the text of the Treaty and signed on behalf of the Principal Allied and Associated Powers by M. Millerand, President of the Peace Conference. The text of this promise is as follows:

"As regards the enclaves of Magyar population which will pass under another sovereignty, the treaties for the protection of minorities already signed provide them with a full safeguard."

I must, therefore, ask the Assembly, on behalf of Hungary, for an effective protection of minorities. I shall not propose any new procedure for the reorganization of this protection, since I consider that this question is one for the great Powers which signed the Minorities Treaties, and we cannot suppose that they desire to abolish or even to weaken the system of the protection of minorities based on moral principles.

For these reasons I do not wish to express an opinion on the Polish contention concerning the generalization of obligations for the protection of minorities. I only wish to state our conviction that, whether or not these obligations are generalized in the future, no decision that is taken can abolish or even weaken, as regards the Hungarian minorities, the stipulations of the treaties in force. In Hungary's case, the protection promised to the Hungarian minority, and the international supervision of this protection, constituted the conditions of the transfer of considerable territories to the Successor States; hence respect for this essential condition is closely bound up with other questions of very considerable importance.

My task here as delegate of Hungary simply consists in speaking to you of the more effective application of the already existing stipulations of the Minorities Treaties.

My first duty is to express my gratitude to the organs of the League which deal with the protection of minorities and to thank them for continuing, in increasingly difficult circumstances, to display the utmost goodwill and the most generous zeal in the service of a lofty ideal. The situation which I must briefly describe to you is nevertheless extremely grave. In saying this I have no desire to lay the responsibility at the door of the competent organs of the League of Nations. But it is none the less true that, in the times in which we are living, the "vulpine intellect" so severely criticised and so energetically combated by the great British historian Carlyle is again beginning to gain the upper hand.

In his opening speech to the Assembly, the President of the Council, His Excellency M. Benes, carefully reviewed the "debit items in the League's balance-sheet for the past year." I regret that he should have omitted to mention the greatest debit item, the decadence of the protection of minorities, and that he did not draw the Assembly's attention from the Presidential chair to the disquieting situation which has resulted. The most serious symptom of this situation seems to me to be the tendency, which has been very evident in recent times, to neglect and infringe to an ever greater extent the stipulations of the Minorities Treaties, described as sacred by Mr. de Valera. These treaties cannot, however, be allowed to remain a dead letter. The protection of minorities must be a living reality and, for these minorities themselves, it is much more important even than the formal recognition of the treaties which instituted it.

There are countries which are not bound by any treaty, but in which a perfect equality of rights nevertheless exists.

Switzerland, which stands so high in our esteem and which offers us such generous hospitality, has for centuries been a model in this respect. Another example is Luxemburg, a still smaller country in size, but a great one in moral standing, whose population enjoys absolute liberty and a full and harmonious life, with a trilingual system which might well be taken as a model by many countries which have always been or have become larger.

Other countries, again, have solemnly accepted the supervision of the protection of minorities in order to obtain large accessions of territory; but, instead of protecting their minorities, they systematically oppress them and thus rendder the League's guarantee illusory. This attitude constitutes a serious threat to good relations between neighbouring countries and to the peace of Europe. The very foundation of the League of Nations—namely, respect for the obligations that have been assumed, including those regarding the protection of the minorities—may be shaken. Instead of the principles of humanity and morality which should reign in an advanced civilization like our own, the primitive principle of the right of the strongest is allowed to triumph. The strongest in relation to the minority is always the national majority, which, if it wishes, can unscrupulously impose upon the minority its most selfish interests.

If the problem is examined, it will be seen that it is chiefly in Central Europe that the protection of minorities is undergoing rapid and progressive decadence. As it is in Roumania, where more than half of the annexed Hungarian population lives, that the situation of the minorities has become particularly difficult and even untenable, I propose to describe to you the real facts as they have been for sev-

eral years past, and to compare these facts with the stipulations of the Treaty of Paris. In that country, to which
the Treaty of Trianon granted more former Hungarian
territory than it left to Hungary, you will see for yourselves how each article of the treaty concluded with a view
to ensuring protection of minorities has been violated point
by point. The protection of minorities has been transformed
into the persecution of minorities. The Treaty of Paris no
longer exists and discriminatory treatment pushed to the
extreme has reached a maximum. Each article of the Treaty
of Paris has been infringed; the Treaty has become a
"scrap of paper." I shall show you what the real situation
is in the light of the eleven articles of the treaty, in order
that you may be able to realize for yourselves the gravity
of the position and that you may be able to draw just conclusions with a view to that more effective protection of
minorities which is so necessary.

And yet, in signing the Treaty of Paris for the protection
of minorities, Roumania undertook to observe its provisions. To do this she ought, according to the formal stipulations contained in Article I, to have inserted in the fundamental laws of the state the provisions of the Minorities
Treaty and to have rendered them obligatory for all her
nationals and for all the organs of the state. Not only has
she not done so, but she has enacted laws contrary to the
Minorities Treaty, such as the law on Roumanian nationality, the constitutional law and the administrative law
placing the minority churches in a state of inferiority
towards the Roumanian National Church, several clauses
of the laws on private education and on elementary education which evade the obligations regarding the teaching of

children in their own language; lastly, we have the "cultural zone" created by the law on elementary education which aims at the Roumanianization of territories of Hungarian language.

Article 2, paragraph I, stipulates the protection of life and liberty which, according to the universally recognised legal principle, implies that of the right of property. But the pillage and outrages committed in December 1928 and May 1933 against the lives and properties of Hungarians in Roumania, the confiscation of private property like that of the Roman Catholic diocese of Transylvania and, quite recently, that of the Piarists and of the Friars Minor on the pretext that it was State property, and the occupation by the Roumanian Government without any compensation of over 200 school buildings belonging to the confessions of the Hungarian minority all constitute breaches of this article.

Paragraph 2 of the same Article 2 stipulates freedom of worship. This freedom, however, is infringed by the Roumanian law on the general regime of public worship, which pronounces against the minority churches provisions suggested by a spirit of petty tyranny, establishes an excessive right of supervision and interference, renders the settlement of internal ecclesiastical affairs subject to the Government approval, and places all kinds of obstacles in the way of the recognition of civil personality. The Unitarian Convention had been summoned to meet this month at Duca. All the participants had already assembled and the first meeting was just about to open when an order arrived from the Minister of the Interior prohibiting the meeting, which was subsequently dissolved by the gendarmerie. According to Roumanian law, however, the administrative meetings of the churches are not subject to previous authorization.

Articles 3 to 7 of the Treaty of Paris grant Roumanian nationality ipso facto to all persons domiciled in Roumania at the time that treaty came into force. The Roumanian law on nationality (Article 56), however, only grants the status of Roumanian national to those resident in Roumanian territory on November 18th, 1918. In addition, it lays down such complicated formalities that even persons who ought automatically to acquire Roumanian nationality are incapable of fulfilling them. As a result of these inequitable requirements, there are tens of thousands of persons of Hungarian language who are entitled to Roumanian nationality but are refused it. As an example, it may be mentioned that, out of 88,000 inhabitants at Oradea, 32,000 have not been entered on the register of Roumanian nationals.

This uncertainty very often comprises the material subsistence of those concerned. They cannot obtain passports or the papers necessary for marrying. If they are public officials they lose their posts and are often threatened with expulsion. Cases might be mentioned in which persons belonging to a minority and of doubtful nationality have been turned back on innumerable occasions on both sides of the frontier.

Last year (1933), the Roumanian Government put into force a system which leaves even more room for arbitrary action and abuses. By unilateral action it is withdrawing Roumanian nationality from persons already legally entered on the register of nationals who were born in Transylvania, who are living there with their families and who possess houses and other immovable property there, and is obliging them to cross the frontier. To our knowledge, victims of this treatment have brought their complaints even before the Council of the League.

Article 8 of the Treaty of Paris recognises equality of civil and political rights; but, in fact, equality exists in Roumania only in theory. As regards civil rights, indeed, the Roumanian Government very often restricts the right of association or of assembly in the case of minority citizens. For example, it has even refused to grant legal personality to the Hungarian League of Nations Union of Roumania. As regards political rights, it is opposed to the free operation of the majority principle, which would be favourable to the Hungarians, in all towns, communes or departments where there is a Hungarian majority. Even in the Szekler area, where the Hungarians form a compact block of half a million inhabitants, there is not a single Hungarian mayor. In the municipal, communal and departmental councils, measures of constraint are taken to ensure a Roumanian majority. With very rare exceptions, public employment is not open to persons belonging to the Hungarian minority, nor do they enjoy the protection which the State owes to all its subjects. For example, when a final judgment has been given in favour of a Hungarian party, it is often not enforced because the administrative authorities refuse their assistance for its enforcement.

Article 8 of the treaty also prohibits any restriction on the free use of any language in commerce or in private intercourse, and yet in some towns signboards in Hungarian are liable to a higher tax than those in Roumanian. Roumanian alone may be employed for trade-marks, and the censorship forbids to use Hungarian place-names. Since

1933, even Hungarian athletic societies have had to give themselves a Roumanian name and to conduct their correspondence in Roumanian. There is a law imposing a tax of 10 per cent on the gross receipts from tickets for theatres giving performances in Roumanian, whereas for performances in other languages the tax is 26 per cent. Lastly, and once again despite the formal provisions of the treaty, the Roumanian courts of law do not accept any application worded in Hungarian.

I now come to Articles 9 and 10, which deal with schools and other minority institutions.

Until 1868, all the schools in Hungary were maintained by the churches. This age-long right of the churches had been confirmed by the old Treaties of Vienna and Linz, and some years later, in 1648, it was placed under international guarantee by the Peace of Westphalia. Accordingly, in view of the transfer of large areas of Hungarian territory to Roumania, the Minorities Treaty seeks to secure the established position of denominational schools which have been in existence for centuries.

Article 9, in particular, assures the minorities of the same treatment and security as the other Roumanian nationals. Its primary object is to guarantee the freedom of education and to enable the minorities, not merely—as is natural enough—to gain instruction and knowledge, but to do so in their own language. The Roumanian State has undertaken to set up minority schools wherever there is a considerable proportion of Roumanian nationals of other than Roumanian speech. Moreover, the treaty gives the minorities themselves the right to establish and direct at their own expense, schools in which instruction shall be given in their own language.

But the Roumanian State has not merely failed to per-
form its undertaking to establish minority schools, but is
opening elementary schools in which instruction is given
in the Roumanian language in the Szekler area, where practically the whole of the population is Hungarian. Compulsory entries, analysis of surnames, educational fines—anything will do to force children to transfer from the minority
schools to the Roumanian-speaking State schools; nothing
is neglected that may help denationalize, to Roumanianize,
the people.

To illustrate the extent to which the Roumanian Government is failing to discharge its obligations, we need only
mention that, in forty-nine towns in Transylvania, where
the proportion of Hungarians is 63 per cent and where
there were 68,000 children of school age in the year 1932–
1933, only 16,000 children—24 per cent—were able to
attend the Hungarian denominational schools, because the
number of children who might be admitted had been limited to that figure by the State. Indeed, the great majority
of these children were deprived of any education whatever. There are some towns, such as Huedin (Bánffy-
Hunyad), where there is not a single Hungarian-speaking
denominational school, although 90 per cent of the population speak Hungarian.

Moreover, the communes inhabited by minorities have to
defray the cost of building and upkeep of Roumanian-
speaking State schools which are entirely superfluous in
those communes. Hence the minorities pay twice their share
of the educational expenses.

The minorities are also unable to exercise the right—
guaranteed though it is by the Treaty of Paris—to establish and maintain at their own expense schools giving in-

struction in their own language. The Roumanian Government grants or withholds, as it thinks fit, permission to open a minority school, and, although no such distinction is known to the Minorities Treaty, the Roumanian law on private education prohibits the minorities from establishing denominational Hungarian-speaking higher schools or training colleges for elementary-school teachers.

Again, where minority schools are still in existence, the law does not recognize them as public institutions; in other words, they cannot issue certificates equivalent to those issued by the State schools. In exceptional cases, the Minister may confer the status of public institutions on these schools; but he frequently withdraws that status without giving any reason. Among other cases, this was done to the Hungarian secondary school of the Friars Minor at Arad in August 1934.

Admission to the denominational schools is frequently made dependent, not on the children's native language—the only criterion mentioned even in the Roumanian law on private education—but on the alleged racial origin, judged by religion, or on an analysis of the surname. Thus, what is called the "objective" method—that is to say, in actual fact, State intervention—displaces national consciousness and parental free will.

It is only in quite exceptional cases that the Roumanian Government authorizes the opening of infant schools, but it organizes a large number of such schools in which instruction is given in Roumanian and which are set up at the expense of the various communes in the Hungarian-Székler departments. The schools-mistresses which it sends there are, as a general rule, ignorant of Hungarian and can, therefore, be of no use to the small children entrusted to their care. In thirty communes of the Comitat of Ciuc, the Hungarian inhabitants of which represent 90 per cent of the total population, there are sixty-three infant schools in which instruction is given in the Roumanian language and not one single State infant or elementary school giving instruction in Hungarian.

One particularly serious grievance has its origin in Article 159 of the Law on Primary Education, under which a so-called cultural zone designed to bring about the Roumanianization of the Hungarians—as is stated quite openly —has been set up in nine predominantly Hungarian departments, in three of which the population is exclusively Hungarian. In that zone, school-teachers sent from the former Kingdom of Roumania, and without the slightest knowledge of Hungarian, are granted special privileges by the State.

The provisions of the "Serviciul local de Invatamant Cluj," dated August 20, 1934, are particularly revolting —I can use no other word. That instrument provides that all religious instruction is to be given exclusively in the official language of the State to enable the supervisory authorities to carry out their duties. This provision prevents the minority pupils from learning the rudiments of their religion, and even their prayers, in their mother tongue.

The Roumanian State budget very creditably provides a subsidy of several million lei for Roumanian schools outside Roumania; but the Roumanian State evades its international obligation to assist minority schools in its own territories.

The Roumanian Law of July 1, 1930, introduced a school tax of 14 per cent; but the Hungarian schools receive nothing out of its proceeds, although, in the Hungarian-Szekler territory, the tax is almost exclusively paid by Hungarians.

Article 9 of the Treaty of Paris for the protection of minorities guarantees to the minorities the right to establish, manage and control, at their own expense, charitable and social institutions. These international legal provisions are likewise infringed by the Roumanian Government.

And to conclude, let me quote Article II of the Minorities Treaty, which reads as follows:

"Roumania agrees to accord to the communities of the Saxons and Szeklers in Transylvania local autonomy in regard to scholastic and religious matters, subject to the control of the Roumanian State."

Fifteen years have now elapsed since the signature of the treaty, and the Roumanian Government has hitherto done nothing to bring such autonomy into effect.

I have given you an account of the position of the Hungarian minorities in Roumania as an example which will enable you to realize the general condition of the minorities in that part of Europe. It is all the more regrettable to note how far the situation has deteriorated and disputes increased in recent years, because the general position in the Danube Basin is, in any case, far from satisfactory, and because it is essential in that part of Europe above all others to obviate new difficulties. The dismemberment of the economic unit formed by the Danube Basin, and the creation of a number of small self-contained units, has had serious consequences which have been still further accentuated by the discrimination between victors and vanquished arising out of the Treaties of Peace.

To this economic and political dislocation must be added the constantly increasing grievances of the minorities. The lamentations of peasants faced with ruin, of the churches and religious orders illegally despoiled of their property, of thousands of school children deprived of their schools, and of officials dismissed from their posts, are heard with increasing frequency, even beyond the frontiers, filling us with alarm and wringing our hearts.

This is not the first time that the position in the Danube Basin, which is the outcome of serious blunders, has claimed the attention of the League of Nations. His Excellency the Roumanian Minister for Foreign Affairs, who enjoys such a distinguished place in the councils of the League, has proposed, as a remedy, that the Customs frontiers should gradually be abolished and present obstacles between the various countries eliminated—in other words, that, as he himself said, the frontiers "should be spiritualized." Allow me then to show you the first step towards the solution which M. Titulesco has proposed to us—a step which it is essential to take if it is seriously desired to embark on the course he has outlined. If the Roumanian Minister for Foreign Affairs is really anxious to eliminate the obstacles which stand in the way of the co-operation between Danubian States, his Government must begin by eliminating the differences which laws, decrees and administrative measures are constantly establishing between the citizens of Roumania herself.

If the Roumanian Foreign Minister wishes to "spiritualize" the political frontiers, it will be necessary to begin by "spiritualizing" the internal barriers, of the existence of which he cannot but be aware, between the citizens of different nationalities within his own country. Respect for undertakings already given, and conduct in keeping with such undertakings, would be infinitely more valuable than the constant reiteration of even the loftiest principle. What Hungary asks of her neighbor is the loyal application of the Minorities Treaties, but that, in the very nature of things, depends upon Roumania alone, and it is she alone who is in a position to take the first step.

For Europe, the last two decades have been a period of war and crises. The conflicts of the battlefields are over, but in one form or another the crisis is still with us and the world is unable to recover its equilibrium. In more than one respect the present position recalls the period of the Thirty Years' War, when religious struggles threatened to plunge the whole of Europe into ruin. So far from appeasing differences, the strife and bloodshed, the terrible sacrifices of that period only served to render them more acute. It was not until thirty years had elapsed that the Peace of Westphalia put an end to the hostilities. That settlement which brought about a genuine peace was, as everyone is aware, the result, not of violence, but of a better and deeper understanding of things. Since that time, religious wars have ceased, not because one of the parties succeeded in imposing its wishes on the other, but, on the contrary, because neither of them attempted to convert its opponents by force. A new international conscience came into being asserting religious freedom, and, instead of striving against the other, the opposing parties united in defense of that noble principle. It is for that reason that the epoch of religious wars is finally closed.

The first decades of the twentieth century have witnessed the emergence in Europe of national differences similar to the religious differences of the seventeenth century. In spite of the world war, these national differences still subsist; but they are no more capable of settlement by arms than the religious differences which preceded them. It is not by force that Europe will find peace, but through the advent of a calmer and more constructive outlook, of higher moral principles, of a new world conscience. The League of Nations, in whose precincts I have the honour to address you in the name of Hungary, is in itself a creation of that higher and more generous world conscience, and no manner of reaction can now prevent the complete triumph of the principles on which the system of the League of Nations is founded.

As yet, indeed, the world conscience of which I have spoken is not sufficiently effective; it is too timid because its working is impeded by all too numerous obstacles which distorted and exacerbated nationalism is placing in its way on every side. That is why it cannot too often be repeated that, intelligently understood, the national idea can never lead to oppression. A civilized nation can never become a prison to its own minorities. A civilized nation is a factor in world organization and its mission is to enrich the human community by the contribution of its own intrinsic values and individual qualities. So far from finding a sufficient outlet in the oppression of other peoples or national minorities, an enlightened nationalism which really respects itself will not begrudge them the respect due to the worth and individuality of all nations. Such constructive nationalism pursues its ends, not through the oppression of others, but through the full and ample development of its own creative forces.

The national policy of Hungary is based upon those principles, and it is those principles which we desire to represent before the League of Nations. But, at the same time, Hungary has the right, and even the duty, to ask that they should also be applied to every Hungarian in whatever country he may be living.

In conjuring up this picture of a somewhat gloomy situation, it is not my intention to create new disputes, but rather to help in remedying the evil and in establishing its causes. Hungary claims nothing that she would not grant to others of her own accord. We ask for nothing new, nothing exceptional. We merely demand the execution of existing undertakings. We claim no new rights, we merely ask for the application of all of that moral law which is binding upon every individual and every nation of goodwill.

We have done our duty by showing what the situation really is. In conclusion, and with the fullest confidence that our plea will be heard, we ask the peoples of the world to put an end to these evils and to forestall the dangers to which they might lead. This intolerable situation has brought the Hungarian Government to realize that its primary duty, both to its own people and to mankind at large, is to do everything in its power to ensure the effective protection of the Hungarian minorities as laid down in international treaties. It is, therefore, determined to continue in its reliance upon the methods of international law, and to that end to avail itself without delay of all the possibilities open to it under the Covenant and the Treaty of Trianon.

Appendix 5

TRANSYLVANIA'S SITUATION IN HUNGARY AND IN EUROPE

BY COUNT PAUL TELEKI*

EVERY REGION of our earth's surface is an individual entity with respect both to space and to time. With respect to space it is a unique piece of earth unlike any other. With respect to time it is a population area of ever-changing character, modified by the common conditions of life of the various periods in the development of our earth's surface and also by the varying requirements of the peoples of the several historical ages. For man, in every regional entity there are elements of stability due to its situation and character and the relative value of changing preponderance.

The surface of the earth is not merely an area of space. It is itself a unique, yet steadily changing entity—an organism living in its parts the continents and seas. These are also individual entities owing to the diversity of their age, size, character, situation, climate and the conditions of life developing as a result of climate. Rich and poor spaces or areas—of varying significance to the men of various periods—form the living and breathing chessboard of the

* Published in Erdely, Kidja a Magyar Tortenelmi Tarsulat, Budapest, 1940 and appearing here for the first time in English.

earth's surface; areas which formerly figured in succession as "worlds" of their own.

Europe is a great population area of this kind—in olden times figuring as a world in itself and subsequently acting for centuries as a world-forming center. Today it has become a part of the total world in balance with population areas of equal or growing importance. A densely populated continent, surrounded and isolated by the seas, by cold and warm steppes, deserts and relatively uninhabited territories, Europe was compelled in the past—and is compelled today—to develop within its boundaries, a symbiosis of human beings and of peoples—a symbiosis of an intimate character made continually richer and stronger by the increase of the density of population and by the increasing communications. The oceanic regions of Central and Western Europe form the greater and more densely populated nucleus of this population area.

This is the real, the true Europe, distinguished from all other great population areas of the world by its highly articulated coast-line and surface, by the mean character and the multifariousness of its surface-forms, and by its great variety with respect to the origin, homelands, languages and manners of its inhabitants. Europe is a unit creating its own form of life, which in the course of its development must of necessity become a single community in labour and thought, at all times in keeping with its physically given fundamental character and with the multifariousness which shapes the kaleidoscopic and stimulating variety of its intellectual development. This highly articulated Europe, with its active brain and its power of intellectual initiative, has its eastern limit behind the eastern fringe of the Baltic Sea, at Lake Ladoga, at the eastern slope of the arc of the Carpathians, and between the open coastal regions and the closed hinterland of the Balkan Peninsula. Europe stretches even beyond these frontier regions, though over bordering districts which are quite different in type from its fundamental character and serve both as settlement areas for the West and as breakwaters against inroads from the East.

When comparing it with the other great population areas of the world, we may speak of Europe—the real Europe—as a "great population area of small dimensions," in contrast to North America, the typical continent of well defined spaces or regions of great extension. The Great State areas of the smaller "world" we know as Europe, all range in extent from 100,000 or 200,000 square miles—great areas enclosed by the sea and high mountains, as groups of areas held together by cominating regions as the British Isles, the Italian and Iberian Peninsulas, the Middle Danube Basin, the Paris Basin, the German mountain-regions of Central Europe with their cauldrons and limitrophe districts. The centrifugal population area of the Scandinavian mass, with its exceptional unity of character, entitles it indeed to be regarded as a "great population area" in itself. Dovetailed between them, we find transitional regions—regions of passage, regions of mountain-passes, borderlands and seashore regions. All have, or have had, their own States, long or short-lived, as the case may be—the small States of Europe.

The oceanic character of Europe penetrates far inland. The Middle Danube Basin is the only continental "great region" in Europe. The effect of this circumstance is seen in climate and in vegetation, (i.e. in the common conditions of life), in the population (i.e. in history) and in manner of cultivation, (i.e. in economics). The inner part of the basin is the Hungarian Lowlands, for the most part originally poor in trees which through the devastations of the Turkish occupation became more treeless than ever. It is today again richer in trees. This plain and its borderlands are surrounded by thickly wooded mountains. Geologically and botanically, Hungary's regions may be divided into four zones.

The first is the so-called steppe-zone. The second is the zone of oak and mixed forests. These two zones constitute the plains and the hilly districts, or downs. Together they form the region which, in keeping with its character, I would call the steppe-border-region, it being the westernmost "island" of the steppe-border-regions of Southern Russia and of farther off Inner-Asia. The basin being closed, especially on the east, southeast, north and northwest, makes many of its features less pronounced, less extreme in character. Owing to the peculiar character of the basin—e.g. the duration and intensity of the sunlight, which furthers the vitaminosity of fruits and vegetables—other features become more prominent.

The third zone is that of the beech forests, which cover the greater part of our mountains. The fourth is the zone of pine forest. These forest-lands, together with the high pasture-lands of the usually round-headed mountains, form the mountainous area of Hungary.

The basin of the steppe-border-region is divided territorially into three parts by the low hills of Transdanubia and the moderately high hills and mountains in the center of the country. The first part is the Great Lowlands in the center (40,000 square miles, average height 360 feet). The second part is the Lesser Lowlands in the West (10,000 square miles, average height 475 feet). The third part is the Transylvanian Basin in the East (10,500 square miles, average height 1300 feet).

The Magyars, or Hungarians at the close of the period of migrations established in this region a permanent State —its occupations being cattle breeding, fishing and agriculture, and to some extent the cultivation of the vine. They came westward from the border districts of the steppes and forests of the Southern Russia of today. They arrived at a propitious moment. At the time there was no strong, settled State in the Danube Basin likely to frustrate the occupation of the country. But the Europe to the west of Hungary—from Ostmark, the eastern fringe of German lands—was already occupied by firmly settled peoples living in a well-ordered State. The Danube Basin was ready to meet its destiny; and that destiny was fulfilled in a remarkable way. The Magyars came from the East. Their scouts sent in advance "had found the grass and the earth to be good and the country well suited to their kinsmen." They were not a pronouncedly steppe people—no longer what is properly called nomadic. Consequently, the most densely populated principal settlement areas of the Magyars of the ninth, tenth and eleventh centuries—the chief seats of the clans—were situated in the loess and marl districts of the oak and mixed tree forest zone in the eastern section of the Lesser Lowlands, in Transdanubia, (the princely clan,) and in the heart of the Transylvanian tableland.* Land, region and people exerted reciprocal influences. The character of the land maintained the character of the people—the "people of the East," as our people was called by Count Stephen Széchényi, the great reformer of

* Treitz's and Kniezsa's compared maps.

the nineteenth century, to whom his opponent, Kossuth, gave the name of "the greatest Hungarian." The people spread over the country, penetrating into the valleys and basins of the downs and mountainous regions, once more following the course marked out by arable land easy to cultivate and by good valley pastures and meadows. A homeland is the product of the interdependence of land and people. For the word "homeland" is no mere symbol for an ideal concept. A "homeland" is a space or area having a substance—it is a soil in which a form of life is rooted—a region in harmony with the people in which that people easily takes root.

The middle Danube, or Carpathian Basin, is an individual entity like the other "great regions" of Europe already mentioned—indeed in many respects a region of far firmer unity. It has an individuality composed of regions harmoniously complementing one another. It has become the homeland of peoples engaged in agriculture and forestry and pasturage, of lowlanders and mountain-dwellers, of original settlers and later comers and colonists all living together in perfect harmony. These peoples of divergent tongues and manners nevertheless use the same roads, frequent the same markets in many complementary closely united small regions, and share the community of interests of ethnically different individuals and groups. These different peoples become familiar with one another, intermarry, and in many points are of one mind. Here we have one of the pivotal factors underlying the State-idea of St. Stephen, the first King of Hungary—as interpreted time and again by the best sons of our country, and as it must continue to be interpreted.

Open towards the west, the southwest and the south,

closed towards the north, the east and the southeast by the protecting ramparts of the forests, the Carpathians and the Transylvanian Alps, this Hungarian Danube Basin is the greatest single bulwark of Europe for defence against the East—thrust forward as it is between the open Polish plain and the Balkans, with the Eastern Transylvanian spurs watching over and dominating the passage from East Europe to the Balkans. It is a natural fastness defending the West of Europe proper against the essentially foreign "limitrophe" regions, an outpost for the protection of Christianity and European culture, inhabited by a courageous warrior people. Once more a symbiosis of land and people has asserted itself historically—from period to period in European history for the last thousand years.

The Transylvanian Basin, and indeed the whole province of Transylvania, are a copy in miniature of United Hungary, of the region as a whole. It is a copy in miniature also of the historical rôle and the historical fate of Great Hungary—yet a copy enhanced and made more intensive by better possibilities of defence and by a far more advanced situation. It is a copy also of the synthesis of treeless and forest and elevated regions—of the synthesis of their forms of life and peoples as conceived by St. Stephen of Hungary and realized by the Hungarian Princes of Transylvania, the patrons of Hungarian culture and Saxon industry, the Maecenases who encouraged the beginnings of Roumanian culture, the defenders of all liberties and in particular of liberty of conscience.

Transylvania is itself a microcosm—within its small compass endlessly rich in mountains and hills of varying form, in valleys and basins of divergent character. All these small regions are individual homes; their landmarks are the deeply beloved horizons of Saxon cities and villages with their fortified churches; of Magyar towns with their ancient colleges, cathedrals and markets; of big Szekely villages; and of scattered Roumanian settlements or Roumanian villages thickly sown in a compact area. A small spot in the world at large, Transylvania has ever been and still is within itself a veritable cosmos, a self-conscious country, whether as an independent principality or as part of a larger State. The spirit of Transylvania as a unit is particularistic; independence marks the spirit of the regions and their peoples. The greater the political and social, spiritual and economic culture of these peoples, the more virile is their sense of freedom, their desire for liberty. The combination of these tendencies—a desire for liberty, particularism, and a sense of independence reflected in an insistence on the right of self-government—explains the fundamental character of the relations with the mother-country through ten centuries of Hungarian history; from them the small country derived the power and self-consciousness enabling it independently to maintain the Hungarian state-idea and Hungarian liberty during the days of Turkish occupation; and they explain also the power of resistance and the desire for self-government displayed by its minorities during the twenty years of Roumanian rule.

There is a Magyar, a Saxon and also a Roumanian Transylvanianism. Strangers notice this Transylvanianism the moment they enter Transylvania. Transylvanians wear it on their sleeves—to use a Shakespearean phrase. To quote the words of a Transylvanian Saxon, Heinrich Zillich:—
"The Transylvanian soul, of which friends and foes have too much to say, is nothing but a peculiar Transylvanian expression of the cultural conscience kindled by opposi-

tion. . . . Those who fail to recognize the essence owing to domestic political antagonisms—are beyond help. Roumania, too, owed her renaissance to this essence." And Ladislas Ravasz, the Transylvanian who is now Reformed Bishop of Budapest, supplements these statements, finding unity in diversity:—"the root of Transylvanianism is —to tolerate contradictions, trusting that they will balance one another; to be able to accept the resultant of the balance and trust to it the hazard of life."

And Zillich continues:—"The task of Transylvania is to stand sentry at the gateway of the West and afford protection against the East." A part of the West thrust forward into the East: like a battlement that is a part of a fortress and at the same time a fortress in itself! Belonging to the West, securing and keeping its peoples for the West, asserting itself humanly and historically by means of the mission and the sense of its peoples—an outpost of the West: that is Transylvania!

An outpost thrust forward by Nature and history behind and between forests—that is the meaning of the name "Transylvania" (Trans-sylvania), as also of the Hungarian name "Erdély"—"erdö-elve" "forest foreland." This country has a Roman, a medieval Latin, a Hungarian and a German name, and none other. The Roumanians, too, use the Hungarian term in its Roumanized form—"Ardeal." It was not until the invention of the "Daco-Roumanian idea" in the nineteenth century that the name "Transylvania" began to be used in historical science and in literature. It only came into fashion among the people when the country came under Roumanian rule twenty-one years ago.

What are the forests behind which lies "Transylvania?" Beyond round, low, forest-clad mountains lies that province

—the mountains and hills spoken of comprehensively by Hungarian geographers as the Central Range or East Hungarian Island Range. This land of mountains—for the most part ancient, weathered masses—extends over an area some 80 miles wide from West to East, and some 90–100 miles wide from North to South. It is a veritable mountain isle like the Appalachians, but not such a barrier. Bordered on the north and south by two mighty arteries of the network of rivers of the Hungarian Danube Basin connecting Transylvania with the Great Lowlands—by the valleys and regions of the Szamos and the Maros—and separated by them from the lofty mountainous districts rising in the south and far to the north-east. But there is a third natural highway leading from the Great Hungarian Lowlands—at a most important point, through the very heart of the island mountains—into the Transylvanian Basin. "Through" is, however, hardly the correct word: for the road leading over the "Királyhágo" Pass from Nágyvarad to Kolozsvár, upstream along the Sebes Körös and downstream along the Szamos, runs along the northern edge of the high mountains, (the Gyalu Alps, the Ore Mountains of Bihar and of Transylvania), passing between these mountains and the lower heights of the "Szilágyság" hills and downs, the "Meszes," "Réz" and "Bükk" hills on the left bank and the "Lápos" mountains on the right bank of the Szamos. Even the mountain district between the Sebes Körös and the Maros is considerably lower than the Carpathians. The mean height of this elevated part of the Island Mountain District is 300–3900 feet, as against a mean height of 4600–5000 and 5900–6600 feet in the case of the Eastern Carpathians and the Transylvanian Alps respectively. We see, therefore, that the dividing line between the Great Hungarian Lowlands and the Transylvanian Basin is neither so high nor so coherent as the wall formed by the Carpathians. Indeed there has never been any lasting political frontier running along the Island Mountains,* whereas the wall of the Carpathians is the second most ancient unchanged political frontier in Europe —the most permanent in character, having been the Pyrenees in Western Europe, where the formation of well-established States and of definite frontiers was, however, completed centuries earlier than in Eastern Europe.

The Island Mountains possess a changing character. The high flat surface of the Gyalu Alps in its monotony resembles a "peneplain," while the Ore Mountains—Carpathian sandstone, limestone crags, unexpectedly deep gorges—remind us of the most beautiful landscapes of the Carpathians. Yet the greater part of these mountains, too, display gentle formations—large, round tops. As far up as the fringes of the forests and even beyond, these sister mountains are rich in Alpine pastures—richer indeed than the mountains to the south of the Maros and even the Carpathians. That is why we find a broad wedge of Roumanian settlements, packed together in close proximity, stretching from South to North between districts of Magyar or mixed character—as may be seen from ethnographic maps. The low hilly district of the "Szilágyság" lying to the north of the great highroad, in which Roumanian settlements are also to be found† is inhabited by a mixed population of Magyars and Roumanians. It has indeed served the Roumanians as a highway of migration into the hills and the

* Cf. Rónai's map showing the durability of frontiers.
† Cf. The historical maps in this volume, in particular that of Prof. Lullinich.

Magyars as a broad, low-lying gateway of communication between West and East. In a wide, terrace-like valley, the Szamos flows through the region, connecting Hungarian towns and urban districts—Nagybánya, Zsibó, Zilah, Dés.

Dés lies at the point where the river crosses the fringe of the basin. A similar situation is that of Kolozsvár, at a point where the river is smaller, but the road is more important. This road forms the shortest way to the center of the Great Lowlands, and in its passage through the Transylvania Basin likewise touches the richer southern districts. This explains the importance of the situation of Kolozsvár from the point of view both of administration and of trade. It is a natural result of its connection with the central part of Hungary. The importance of the situation of a town is of a relative character. For Roumania, Kolozsvár's importance is rather that of a military depot behind the outpost-towns beyond the mountains—the frontier towns cut off from Hungary for strategic reasons, towns that lie on the outskirts of the Hungarian Lowlands and were doomed to an unhappy lot by the frontier provisions of 1919. Such outpost-towns were bridge-heads commanding the openings of valleys and passes, such as Szatmár on the Szamos, Nagykároly in the vicinity of the Kraszna, Nagyvárad at the entrance to the "Királyhágó" road and, farther south, Arad on the Maros, and, lower to the South, Temesvár. These towns were connected under the Roumanian régime by a military (Rochade) railway running along the frontier over the boundary glacis inhabited by Magyars. This glacis was in 1919 thrust forward in the direction of Hungary to dominate the plain. There is no typical market-town line running round the Transylvania Basin such as we find in the Great Hungarian Lowlands. The towns in the South and East are differently situated.

That Basin may be divided into two distinct sections, the northern half is the so-called "Mezöség" region which is poor in trees. Previous to and during the period of the independent principality in the 16th and 17th centuries, this region was inhabited mostly by Magyars and formed at the same time one of Transylvania's most important granaries. The struggles against the Turk and the wars of independence decimated the Hungarians here too. Roumanians filtered in from the Alpine pastures to take their place. The soil was now less cultivated and became poorer. Even the fish ponds in many small valleys, that since the Bronze Age had been one of the sources of the region's wealth, were allowed to fall into disuse.

The heathland of this region is a district of undulating downs to which a quite peculiar character is lent by the earth-slides and earth-flows of its soft slopes. This was the region in which were bred—particularly on the great estates belonging to old Hungarian families—many of the last and best herds of the white steppe cattle so highly valued as indefatigable draft animals. These farms provided the interior parts of the country with oxen and also bulls of this breed. The Capital of this region, the purely market-town Marosvásárhely, its name denotes its market character, lies in the south-east, where the great river of Transylvania, the Maros, coming from the frontier basins of Székelyland enters the great Transylvanian Basin, and is in the vicinity of the richer southern valley districts of the Basin.

These valley districts are formed by the rivers Maros,

Nyárád, Kis Küküllö and Nagy Küküllö, flowing parallel to one another from east-northeast to west-southwest. They are wide, terraced valleys, their northern slopes steeper and their southern slopes gentler in character. The horizontal argillaceous layers have not remained in their original position, having received deposits of rock salt which under the pressure of the other strata shifted like glacial ice, in particular towards the border regions where the pressure was less. There this salt has become massed in compressed and folded blocks. Very ancient salt-mines—Désakna, Kolozs, Torda, Marosujvár, Vizakna, Parajd—are ranged along the fringes of the Transylvanian Basin. Within this zone is the rich natural gas region discovered just prior to the first Great War. The larger towns of the southern half of the Great Transylvanian Basin, the valley districts, are situated naturally on the banks of the rivers, Nagyeneed and Gyulafehérvár on the Maros, Dicsöszentmarton on the Kis Küküllö, Segesvár, Erzsébetváros and Medgyes on the Nagy Küküllö. On the southern fringe of the Basin lies Nagyszeben, near the point where the Olt bends southwards at a point from which this river probably at one time joined the Maros, before it cut its way, perhaps by retrogressive erosion, through the southern mountains. The valley pass leading to Roumania which was brought into being in this way—known as the "Vöröstorony" (Red Tower) Pass—the Olt valley leading eastwards and the ancient depression leading to the Maros at the western gateway of which lies Szászsebes—all explain the importance of Nagyszeben's position and also why the town is so strongly fortified.

In the South, the Transylvanian Basin is enclosed by the highest mountains of the country, being enclosed to the

east of the point at which the Olt has broken through by
the high ridge of the Fogaras Alps running exactly from
east to west, and on the west by crystalline blocks rising to
a height of 6500 feet stretching from the Retyezát to the
mountain-mass of Orsova between which lie mountainous
regions of a lower altitude formed of sedimentary rocks of
a strongly folded character. Between these regions and the
valley of the Lower Maros there rise squat mountains or
hills of an average height of 3200 feet or something more—
Pojana Ruszka, Kudzsir, etc.—just opposite the various
sections of the Central Mountains. The Fogaras range rises
abruptly out of the Fogaras depression on the north edge
of which—a steep ascent—the Olt flows westwards. The
other slope of the Fogaras Alp—the Roumanian one—is
far gentler. Many of the first Roumanian shepherds who
moved northwards from their home in the Balkans must,
after climbing these heights, have obtained from here their
first view of the Basin lying beneath them, then descending
the steep slopes or passing through the "Red Tower" Pass.
Fogaras and valleys of the neighboring mountain districts
situated to the west were also the Transylvanian homes of
the first Roumanian settlers who moved down from the
Alpine pastures and were settled or rather given homes
there by the kings of Hungary.

On the northern shore of the Olt in the Fogaras district
there rises a gradient of some 300 feet only, but very sud-
den and continuous; this was formerly the bastion or line
of defense of the eastern section of the Saxon settlement-
area. From this line, the Saxon area penetrates in a west-
erly direction *via* Nagyszeben far into the valley of the
Maros, stretching northwards almost as far as the Kis
Küküllö and eastwards almost to the foot of the "Hargita"

region—the land of the Székelys, the other frontier people of defense against the East.

The Eastern Carpathians too, like those farther north, are accompanied on their side by a mighty row of volcanic hills. These latter include the "Hargita" (4900–5900 feet), a distinct mountain range, of which the Székely poets sing and to which the soul of the Székelys is so devoted. Together with their continuations in the south and north, the Baróth mountains and the Görgény Alps, they form a mighty wall 90 miles long, rising like a second wall of protection on the easternmost parapet of Transylvania, and simultaneously of Western Europe.

Between these mountains and the outer main line of the Carpathians—the Gyergyó, Csik, Bereck and Brassó Alps, the latter looking southwards—lie four extensive basins, those of Gyergyó, Csik, Háromszék and Brassó. The two northern basins, in which the Maros has its source, are more elevated, genuine mountain basins. The two lying farther south, which are the sources of the tributaries of the Olt, are larger and more open Alpine foreland. The road leads from one basin into the other as far as Brassó in the South, a Saxon town which has become more and more Magyar in character, both because of its position as a market town and because of the constant stream of Székely immigrants, the latter process having continued also during the years of Roumanian rule. Brassó is separated from the Fogaras Basin by a mountain ridge. In the Háromszék Basin there are two chief towns—Sepsiszentgyörgy and Kézdivásárhely—which are, however, much smaller; while in the two mountain basins the prevailing type of settlement is of a quite peculiar character; instead of a large number of smaller townships, there are—especially in Gyergyó—a few large communes fairly equal in size, 5000–10,000 inhabitants, the two principal townships— Csikszereda and Gyergyószentmiklós—playing only the role of "Primi inter pares." The outer mountain wall, average height 5500 feet, behind which lie these four typical reservoir basins of a frontier population, is of international political importance. It commands the gateway which— never broader than 30–40 miles—leads from the Russian lowlands to the Balkans between the easternmost Carpathian spurs and the Danube delta—the gateway of Focsani, the importance of which is stressed by the frontiers and strategic lines that have passed through it in the various periods of history. To the north of the Görgény and Gyergyó Alps, the sandstone and volcanic walls of the Carpathians loom large in close formation, constituting a single, extremely broad bastion rising in places to a height of 7500 feet between Transylvania and Moldavia and Bukovina. These mountains enclose the most north-easterly section of Transylvania, which is the most remote and—until today—economically the least significant—the Besztercze region. Besztercze is a Saxon town, not so beautiful or so typical as those in the southern Saxon region, and is inhabited—like the region itself—by all three of the peoples of Transylvania. The highest mountains, those of Radna, and the ridge of the main wall of the Carpathians, are important watersheds. Through the Naszód Valley, the Nagy Szamos flows into Transylvania; in the North the Iza passes through South Máramaros to join the Upper Tisza: while on the outer edge we find the sources of the Pruth and the Sereth, running to Moldavia. The high mountains, which are here fairly rich in Alpine pasture-land, are again an old focus of Roumanian settlement, in this case of immigration from Moldavia. This accounts for the fact that the Greater Roumania created in 1919 on an exaggerated ethnographical basis advanced far into the territory of Maramaros—as far as the upper reaches of the Tisza—the distinctly Magyar city of Marmarossziget, county seat of the Ruthenian populated Marmaros, lying on the left bank of the Tisza, thus becoming the northernmost town of Roumania.

We might indeed describe the Roumania of today—as contrasted with the concentric Hungary of the Danube Basin—as centrifugal country. The wall of the Carpathians is not only a mighty partition, but only ten passes with an average height of 2800 feet and stretching over a frontier more than 600 miles long lead through them from Transylvania to Roumania. There is also a forest barrier, a zone 30–40 miles wide, practically uninhabited, and crossed by only four railway lines connecting the two countries—Roumania and Transylvania—so divergent in character and culture, even today, in the age of aeroplanes, a dividing zone of this kind is of great significance, as is proved by the Southern Appalachian Mountains, U.S.A. Such separation is always more effectual where the countries are divided and their peoples belong to two different spheres of culture, character and tradition, and are connected with different regions—where each of the countries gravitates in a different direction and follows a different system. Particularly is this the case when the respective networks of markets and systems of small and large towns indivisibly connected, as also the natural routes of communication and the form of settlement resulting from trade by barter, bring these two countries within the magic circles of divergent cultures and manners, and link each one of them respectively to other "great population areas" of the earth. That is what has happened here, too. Not only the settlement-map of Roumania, but also the two large ethnographical maps coloured to show ethnic differences, show clearly enough the intimate connection binding together Transylvania and Hungary proper. All maps, whether geological or orographical, the maps showing the highways of communication, which have remained the same for centuries, and those showing the factors of economic life, which tell us of a unique synthesis—all bear witness to the unity of the Hungarian Basin of the Middle Danube as having a stability which is extremely rare.* The Roumania created by the Berlin Congress is a country forming a connecting link, not between West and East, but between the "great population areas" of Russia and the Balkans, limitrophe regions of Europe. The heart of Roumania is a sinus, thrust forward in a south-westerly direction, of the almost boundless eastern flat land, which advances into the Balkans. Way of living, form of life, culture (Byzantine, as against the Latin-Germanic culture of Western Europe) and tradition are homogeneous in these limitrophe regions and are essentially foreign to the people of Transylvania.

For tradition is by no means merely a myth. Tradition is not merely national. Tradition is the accumulation—the becoming hereditary—of the lifelong and everyday, living common experience of inseparable generations working in intimate cooperation and sharing affections and joining

* Cf. Count Paul Teleki: The Evolution of Hungary and its Place in European History (Williams College Lectures), New York, 1923.

forces for common defense, generations living on the same soil, with the same prospects and horizon. Tradition is an element and an instrument making for conciliation in the eternal struggle against one-sided values and appraisement which continues unceasingly amid the changing conditions of succeeding ages.